Editor
Cristina Krysinski, M. Ed.

Editor in Chief
Karen J. Goldfluss, M.S. Ed.

Creative Director
Sarah M. Fournier

Cover Artist
Barbara Lorseyedi

Art Coordinator
Renée Mc Elwee

Imaging
Amanda R. Harter

Publisher
Mary D. Smith, M.S. Ed.

TCR 8250

M000095451

Comprehending Text
Using Literal, Inferential & Applied Questioning

Twenty texts presented in a variety of genres with activities to reinforce close reading

Related comprehension strategies activities for each unit

Three levels of questioning to improve comprehension and critical-thinking skills

Correlated to the Common Core State Standards

Teacher Created Resources

For correlations to the Common Core State Standards, see page 109 of this book or visit *http://www.teachercreated.com/standards*.

Teacher Created Resources
6421 Industry Way
Westminster, CA 92683
www.teachercreated.com

ISBN: 978-1-4206-8250-2

© 2015 Teacher Created Resources
Made in U.S.A.

Teacher Created Resources

Table of Contents

Introduction

Twenty different texts from a variety of genres are included in this reading comprehension resource. These may include humor, fantasy, myth/legend, folktale, mystery, adventure, suspense, fairy tale, play, fable, science fiction, poetry, and informational/nonfiction texts, such as a timetable, letter, report, procedure, poster, map, program, book cover, and cartoon.

Three levels of questions are used to indicate the reader's comprehension of each text.

One or more particular comprehension strategies have been chosen for practice with each text.

Each unit is five pages long and consists of the following resources and strategies:

- teacher information: includes the answer key and extension suggestions
- text page: text is presented on one full page
- activity page 1: covers literal and inferential questions
- activity page 2: covers applied questions
- applying strategies: focuses on a chosen comprehension strategy/strategies

Teacher Information

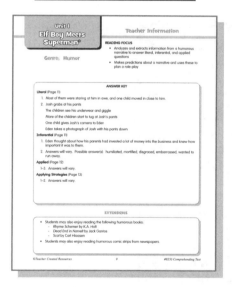

Text Page

- **Reading Focus** states the comprehension skill emphasis for the unit.
- **Genre** is clearly indicated.
- **Answer Key** is provided. For certain questions, answers will vary, but suggested answers are given.
- **Extension Activities** suggest other authors or book titles. Other literacy activities relating to the text are suggested.

- The title of the text is provided.
- Statement is included in regard to the genre.
- Text is presented on a full page.

Activity Page 1

Activity Page 2

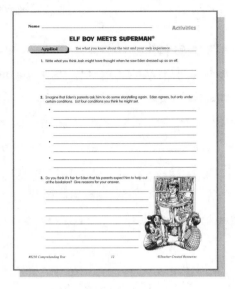

- **Literal** questions provide opportunities to practice locating answers in the text.

- **Inferential** questions provide opportunities to practice finding evidence in the text.

- **Applied** questions provide opportunities to practice applying prior knowledge.

Applying Strategies

- Comprehension strategy focus is clearly labeled.

- Activities provide opportunities to utilize the particular strategy.

Types of Questions

Students are given **three types of questions** (all grouped accordingly) to assess their comprehension of a particular text in each genre:

- **Literal questions** are questions for which answers can be found directly in the text.

- **Inferential questions** are questions for which answers are implied in the text and require the reader to think a bit more deeply about what he or she has just read.

- **Applied questions** are questions that require the reader to think even further about the text and incorporate personal experiences and knowledge to answer them.

Answers for literal questions are always given and may be found on the Teacher Information pages. Answers for inferential questions are given when appropriate. Applied questions are best checked by the teacher following, or in conjunction with, a class discussion.

Comprehension Strategies

Several specific comprehension strategies have been selected for practice in this book.

Although specific examples have been selected, often other strategies, such as scanning, are used in conjunction with those indicated, even though they may not be stated. Rarely does a reader use only a single strategy to comprehend a text.

Strategy Definitions

Predicting	Prediction involves the students using illustrations, text, or background knowledge to help them construct meaning. Students might predict what texts could be about, what could happen, or how characters could act or react. Prediction may occur before, during, and after reading, and it can be adjusted during reading.
Making Connections	Students comprehend texts by linking their prior knowledge with the new information from the text. Students may make connections between the text and themselves, between the new text and other texts previously read, and between the text and real-world experiences.
Comparing	This strategy is closely linked to the strategy of making connections. Students make comparisons by thinking more specifically about the similarities and differences between the connections being made.
Sensory Imaging	Sensory imaging involves students utilizing all five senses to create mental images of passages in the text. Students also use their personal experiences to create these images. The images may help students make predictions, form conclusions, interpret information, and remember details.

Strategy Definitions *(cont.)*

**Determining Importance/
Identifying Main Idea(s)**

The strategy of determining importance is particularly helpful when students try to comprehend informational texts. It involves students determining the important theme or main idea of particular paragraphs or passages.

As students become effective readers, they will constantly ask themselves what is most important in a phrase, sentence, paragraph, chapter, or whole text. To determine importance, students will need to use a variety of information, such as the purpose for reading, their knowledge of the topic, background experiences and beliefs, and understanding of the text format.

Skimming

Skimming is the strategy of looking quickly through texts to gain a general impression or overview of the content. Readers often use this strategy to quickly assess whether a text, or part of it, will meet their purpose. Because this book deals predominantly with comprehension after reading, skimming has not been included as one of the major strategies.

Scanning

Scanning is the strategy of quickly locating specific details, such as dates, places, or names, or those parts of the text that support a particular point of view. Scanning is often used, but not specifically mentioned, when used in conjunction with other strategies.

Synthesizing/Sequencing

Synthesizing is the strategy that enables students to collate a range of information in relation to the text. Students recall information, order details, and piece information together to make sense of the text. Synthesizing/sequencing helps students to monitor their understanding. Synthesizing involves connecting, comparing, determining importance, posing questions, and creating images.

Summarizing/Paraphrasing

Summarizing involves the processes of recording key ideas, main points, or the most important information from a text. Summarizing or paraphrasing reduces a larger piece of text to the most important details.

Genre Definitions

Fiction and Poetry

Science Fiction These stories include backgrounds or plots based upon possible technology or inventions, experimental medicine, life in the future, environments drastically changed, alien races, space travel, genetic engineering, dimensional portals, or changed scientific principles. Science fiction encourages readers to suspend some of their disbelief and examine alternate possibilities.

Suspense Stories of suspense aim to make the reader feel fear, disgust, or uncertainty. Many suspense stories have become classics. These include *Frankenstein* by Mary Shelley, *Dracula* by Bram Stoker, and *Dr. Jekyll and Mr. Hyde* by Robert Louis Stevenson.

Mystery Stories from this genre focus on the solving of a mystery. Plots of mysteries often revolve around a crime. The hero must solve the mystery, overcoming unknown forces or enemies. Stories about detectives, police, private investigators, amateur sleuths, spies, thrillers, and courtroom dramas usually fall into this genre.

Fable A fable is a short story that states a moral. Fables often use talking animals or animated objects as the main characters. The interaction of the animals or animated objects reveals general truths about human nature.

Fairy Tale These tales are usually about elves, dragons, goblins, fairies, or magical beings and are often set in the distant past. Fairy tales usually begin with the phrase "Once upon a time . . ." and end with the words ". . . and they lived happily ever after." Charms, disguises, and talking animals may also appear in fairy tales.

Fantasy A fantasy may be any text or story that is removed from reality. Stories may be set in nonexistent worlds, such as an elf kingdom, on another planet, or in alternate versions of the known world. The characters may not be human (dragons, trolls, etc.) or may be humans who interact with non-human characters.

Folktale Stories that have been passed from one generation to the next by word of mouth rather than by written form are folktales. Folktales may include sayings, superstitions, social rituals, legends, or lore about the weather, animals, or plants.

Play Plays are specific pieces of drama, usually enacted on a stage by actors dressed in makeup and appropriate costumes.

Adventure Exciting events and actions feature in these stories. Character development, themes, or symbolism are not as important as the actions or events in an adventure story.

Humor Humor involves characters or events that promote laughter, pleasure, or humor in the reader.

Genre Definitions *(cont.)*

Fiction and Poetry *(cont.)*

Poetry	This genre utilizes rhythmic patterns of language. The patterns include meter (high- and low-stressed syllables), syllabication (the number of syllables in each line), rhyme, alliteration, or a combination of these. Poems often use figurative language.
Myth	A myth explains a belief, practice, or natural phenomenon and usually involves gods, demons, or supernatural beings. A myth does not necessarily have a basis in fact or a natural explanation.
Legend	Legends are told as though the events were actual historical events. Legends may or may not be based on an elaborated version of a historical event. Legends are usually about human beings, although gods may intervene in some way throughout the story.

Nonfiction

Journalistic Writing	Usually formal and structured, journalistic writing aims to present information accurately, clearly, and efficiently rather than to present and develop an individual writer's style. Journalistic writing is usually written in the third person.
Letter	These are written conversations sent from one person to another. Letters usually begin with a greeting, contain the information to be related, and conclude with a farewell signed by the sender.
Report	Reports are written documents describing the findings of an individual or group. They may take the form of a newspaper report, sports report, or police report, or a report about an animal, person, or object.
Biography	A biography is an account of a person's life written by another person. The biography may be about the life of a celebrity or a historical figure.
Autobiography	An autobiography is a piece of writing in which a writer uses his/her own life as the basis for a biography.
Journal	A journal is a continued series of texts written by a person about his/her life experiences and events. Journals may include descriptions of daily events as well as thoughts and emotions.
Diary	A diary contains a description of daily events in a person's life.

Other **informational texts**, such as **timetables**, are excellent sources to teach and assess comprehension skills. Others may include **diagrams, graphs, advertisements, maps, plans, tables, charts, lists, posters,** and **programs**.

Genre: Humor

READING FOCUS

- Analyzes and extracts information from a humorous narrative to answer literal, inferential, and applied questions
- Makes predictions about a narrative and uses these to plan a role-play

ANSWER KEY

Literal (Page 11)

1. Most of them were staring at him in awe, and one child moved in close to him.

2. Josh grabs at his pants

   The children see his underwear and giggle

   More of the children start to tug at Josh's pants

   One child gives Josh's camera to Eden

   Eden takes a photograph of Josh with his pants down

Inferential (Page 11)

1. Eden thought about how his parents had invested a lot of money into the business and knew how important it was to them.

2. Answers will vary. Possible answer(s): humiliated, mortified, disgraced, embarrassed, wanted to run away.

Applied (Page 12)

1–3. Answers will vary.

Applying Strategies (Page 13)

1–2. Answers will vary.

EXTENSIONS

- Students may also enjoy reading the following humorous books:
  - *Rhyme Schemer* by K.A. Holt
  - *Dead End in Norvelt* by Jack Gantos
  - *Scat* by Carl Hiaasen
- Students may also enjoy reading humorous comic strips from newspapers.

ELF BOY MEETS SUPERMAN®

Name _____

Read the humorous narrative and answer the questions on the following pages.

Yesterday started out as the worst day of my life.

"But Mom, I can't do it. I just can't."

"Please, Eden. We need you."

I sighed. If it wasn't bad enough that Mom and Dad had bought a children's bookstore, now they expected me to help out. Hadn't they done enough to ruin my life? Try having a unique name like Eden. It would be bad enough for a girl, but for a boy, it's a disaster.

I tried again. "Mom, 12-year-old boys just don't dress up like elves and tell stories to little kids. What if someone sees me?"

"Eden, I wouldn't ask you if it wasn't important. There's no one else who can do it. The actor we hired called in sick. Besides, you're so good at drama."

Mom's face was anxious. I knew she and Dad had invested a lot of money into buying the business. But what if someone from school saw me? I glanced at the customers and saw only little kids and their parents.

So the next thing I knew, I was dressed in a green felt costume, sitting in the corner of the store in front of a bunch of four-year-olds. I drew the line and refused to wear the red-striped socks, but I was wearing the sparkly shoes. I felt ridiculous, so I began the story as soon as I could. I used different voices for the characters, and the kids really seemed to like it. Most of them were staring up at me in awe. One kid even moved so close he was half-sitting on my foot. With only a page to go, I was beginning to feel relieved. It was almost over. But a sentence away from the end, I glanced up—and looked straight into the eyes of Josh Baxter, the toughest kid in my school. My mouth dried up, and I froze.

"Hi, Eden," he snickered. "Or should I say 'Elf Boy'? Nice outfit."

I jumped to my feet and tried to think of something to say. Meanwhile, Josh was digging in his backpack. Before I could do anything, he'd whipped out a digital camera.

"I think everyone at school would like to see Eden the Elf Boy, don't you?"

I wanted to run, but I couldn't. I was surrounded by little kids.

Then, one of the boys stood up and tugged at Josh's pants. "Leave Mr. Elf alone, you meanie. He hasn't finished the story."

Josh just ignored the kid and aimed the camera at me. But the boy kept tugging at Josh's pants. They were quite loose, and they started to slide down. Josh realized what was happening and had to grab his pants with his free hand. But it was too late. The children had seen his underwear, and they started to giggle. Before I knew what was happening, more of them had jumped up and began to tug at Josh's pants. While he tried to swat them away, one of them grabbed the camera and handed it to me. Just as Josh's pants reached his ankles, I snapped the perfect picture of him in his Superman® underwear. He yelped, pulled up his sweatpants, and charged out of the store, with all the customers staring and laughing.

Yesterday started out as the worst day of my life, but it ended up pretty well. I actually quite enjoyed my day as an elf. And I've got photographic evidence that Superman® exists.

ELF BOY MEETS SUPERMAN®

Literal   Find the answers directly in the text.

1. What made Eden think that the children liked his storytelling?

_____

_____

2. Complete the chain of events that led to Josh leaving the shop.

   • *Josh's pants start to slide down* _____

   • _____

   • _____

   • _____

   • _____

   • _____

   • *Josh runs out of the shop* _____

Inferential   Think about what the text says.

1. Most likely, why did Eden agree to do the storytelling?

_____

_____

_____

2. List some words and phrases that describe how Eden may have felt when Josh first approached him.

_____

_____

_____

Name _____

ELF BOY MEETS SUPERMAN®

Applied   Use what you know about the text and your own experience.

1. Write what you think Josh might have thought when he saw Eden dressed up as an elf.

_____

_____

_____

2. Imagine that Eden's parents ask him to do some storytelling again. Eden agrees, but only under certain conditions. List four conditions you think he might set.

- _____

- _____

- _____

- _____

3. Do you think it's fair for Eden that his parents expect him to help out at the bookstore? Give reasons for your answer.

_____

_____

_____

_____

_____

_____

_____

ELF BOY MEETS SUPERMAN®

Predicting

Think about the characters of Eden and Josh from the humorous text on page 10 to make some predictions.

1.

	Eden	Josh
Predict what this character might do immediately after the story ends.		
Predict what this character might do that night.		
Predict what this character might do before school the next morning.		

2. Find a partner and discuss both sets of predictions. Circle the ones you like the most. Use these to help you plan and present a humorous role-play that takes place when the characters see each other the next day at school. You can change the names and gender of the characters if you need to (e.g., "Josh" could become "Jacinta").

    a. Where does the scene take place? _____

    _____

    b. How does the scene start? _____

    _____

    c. How does the scene end? _____

    _____

3. Practice your role-play. When you are ready, present it to a small group or to the class.

Unit 2
Between Outer-Earth and Inner-Earth

Genre: Fantasy

READING FOCUS

- Analyzes and extracts information from a fantasy to answer literal, inferential, and applied questions
- Predicts and makes connections to show comprehension of a text

---

ANSWER KEY

Literal (Page 16)

1. True   2. False   3. False   4. True   5. False

Inferential (Page 16)

1. huge, narrowed eyes; sharp claws; and long, greasy hair covered their bodies

2. Sludghe reminded Murrkh that sometimes the place where you are is where you are meant to be.

3. "He walked and walked until his legs and feet would go no farther, rested, then walked again. As time merged from one mega-day into another . . ."

Applied (Page 17)

1–4. Answers will vary.

Applying Strategies (Page 18)

1–2. Answers will vary.

EXTENSIONS

- Other titles in the fantasy genre include the following:
    - *The Mistmantle Chronicles: Urchin of the Riding Stars* by M.I. McAllister
    - *The Chanters of Tremaris* series by Kate Constable
    - *Guardians of Time: The Key* by Marianne Curley
    - *Stravaganza: City of Flowers* by Mary Hoffman
    - *Through the Tiger's Eye* by Kerrie O'Connor

BETWEEN OUTER-EARTH AND INNER-EARTH

Name _____

Read the fantasy story and answer the questions on the following pages.

Another world exists between the polluted atmosphere of the human world and the clean center of Earth. Driven by years of neglect and abuse, a group of humans fled to the between-Earth to escape an inevitable, painful death. These beings evolved into half-human creatures, Pollumants, who only survived by adapting to their dark and colorless world. Huge, narrowed eyes allowed them to see in any light that managed to pierce their gloomy world; sharp claws enabled them to forage for food; and their long, greasy hair covered their bodies to help them to retain body heat.

A rudimentary civilization developed, with each family group dependent on the strongest male to protect, feed, and defend his superiority. Areas were set aside for the disposal of waste, the cultivation of "dark" food, and for living quarters and leisure activities. Male family leaders met together to discuss community problems and concerns.

One such family leader was Murrkh. Murrkh remembered his great-grandfather telling him stories as a little boy about the world above— once green with trees and plants, with clear blue skies providing expanses of air for birds of all descriptions, and sparkling seas teeming with fish.

As Murrkh waited for his time to speak at the community meeting this day, he was anxious and scared. His body shivering and his heart racing as he contemplated the momentous decision he had come to—to venture above the between-Earth into the world above. This was a mission he had often dreamt of doing.

Murrkh announced his request to the head Pollumant, Sludghe, and the assembled family leaders. He waited patiently as loud grumblings and arguments were voiced by one family leader after another. He had expected that his request would be refused, as no Pollumant for many years had ventured outside the between-Earth. Those who had left previously had never returned.

Finally, Sludghe held up his arms for silence and asked Murrkh why he wanted to go.

"I've heard such wondrous tales of the world above, that I feel that I must go to see if it still exists. Otherwise, how will I ever be content with what I have and where I am, if there may be something better above?"

"Very well, Murrkh," said Sludghe. "You have my permission to explore the world above, if it is still there. But remember, that sometimes the place where you are is where you are meant to be."

Murrkh packed his supply of under-water and dark food. Finally, dressed in his cloak, he began his long, silent journey into the world above. He walked and walked until his legs and feet would go no farther, rested, then walked again. As time merged from one mega-day into another, he could gradually discern some lightening of the shadows and shapes ahead. The ground beneath his feet tilted steeply upward, and the pathway narrowed. Soon he had to twist and turn his head and body to maneuver through the rocks. Finally, he dragged himself onto level ground onto an open plain darkly shadowed by black skies and craggy, empty mountains.

As he stared in dismay at the scene before him, a half-human creature with sharp claws, huge narrowed eyes, and a body covered with long, greasy hair came into view . . .

BETWEEN OUTER-EARTH AND INNER-EARTH

Literal   Find the answers directly in the text.

Read each sentence. Decide if each statement is **True** or **False**.

1. The Pollumants were able to develop a basic form of community life.   ☐ True ☐ False

2. Murrkh was an orphan.   ☐ True ☐ False

3. Sludghe wanted to venture outside the between-Earth.   ☐ True ☐ False

4. Murrkh had to prepare for his journey.   ☐ True ☐ False

5. Murrkh did not discover the above world.   ☐ True ☐ False

Inferential   Think about what the text says.

Locate evidence from the text to support each of the following statements.

1. The Pollumants were not entirely human.

   _____

   _____

   _____

2. Sludghe knew that the world above was not any better than the between-Earth.

   _____

   _____

   _____

3. The journey to the world above took a long time.

   _____

   _____

   _____

BETWEEN OUTER-EARTH AND INNER-EARTH

Applied   Use what you know about the text and your own experience.

1. Do you think that Murrkh was pleased when he had discovered the world above? Why or why not?

_____

_____

_____

2. Was the world above better than between-Earth? Why or why not?

_____

_____

_____

3. Is it possible that the world as we know it today could transform into the world described in the text? Why or why not?

_____

_____

_____

_____

4. ". . . otherwise, how will I ever be content with what I have and where I am, if there may be something better above?"

What are your thoughts regarding this excerpt from the text? Do you agree that one cannot be content if he/she believes there is something better?

_____

_____

_____

_____

_____

BETWEEN OUTER-EARTH AND INNER-EARTH

 **Predicting**

This page should be used in conjunction with the text on page 15.

1. Use the lines below to write a short prediction of what may have happened before and after the time frame in the text.

Before   **After**

_____   _____

_____   _____

_____   _____

_____   _____

_____   _____

_____   _____

Making Connections

2. Imagine that the inhabitants of the world above and those of the between-Earth decided to live together using both worlds to live in.

Draw a map of the joined worlds, and write a description of the way each world is used.

_____

_____

_____

_____

_____

_____

_____

_____

_____

READING FOCUS

- Analyzes and extracts information from a diary excerpt to answer literal, inferential, and applied questions
- Uses sensory imaging to assist with the overall understanding of the diary's writer
- Predicts and makes connections to continue a written text

ANSWER KEY

Literal (Page 21)

1. the Northern Districts Annual Medieval Fair
2. crutches
3. the plaster cast on his foot
4. A parachuter in distress blew off course and landed on James.

Inferential (Page 21)

1. Answers will vary. Possible answer(s): accident-prone, humorous, optimistic.
2. Answers will vary.
3. James was at the emergency room. The diary entry mentions a bed, and he talks about wanting to become a doctor. The entry also mentions him getting stitches.

Applied (Page 22)

1. James might be sleeping in the spare room because the location of the spare room might be easier access for those helping to take care of James. His bedroom may be on the second floor.
2. Answers will vary. Possible answer(s):
   Advantages—people are helping you, time to relax
   Disadvantages—rely on others, unable to walk without crutches, unable to play sports, painful
3. Answers will vary.

Applying Strategies (Page 23)

1–2. Answers will vary.

EXTENSIONS

- Students can research the following:
  - events held at medieval festivals
  - the history of the battles reenacted and/or the countries that hold medieval festivals and battle reenactments
- Some titles of literature set in medieval times include the following:
  - *Catherine, Called Birdy* by Karen Cushman
  - *The Midwife's Apprentice* by Karen Cushman
  - *Proud Knight, Fair Lady: The Twelve Lais of Marie de France* translated by Naomi Lewis
  - *A Single Shard* by Linda Sue Park
  - *The Magician's Apprentice* by Sidney and Dorothy Rosen
  - *The Ramsay Scallop* by Frances Temple

Name _____

Read the excerpt from a student's diary and answer the questions on the following pages.

Sunday, February 27

"What a day! In less than ten minutes, it will be "tomorrow," but I'm not ready for sleep yet. If I don't record the events of this remarkable day now, while they're as clear as crystal in my usually befuddled brain, I may believe I dreamt the whole thing and put it down to my overactive imagination. But, hey, that wouldn't be possible ... look at the mountain of evidence to prove it all happened....

Monday, February 28
8:00 a.m.

CD kicked in to rouse me from my slumber. Nothing unusual there, but get this, I'm not here ... in my room, that is. Everything in the room is familiar, you know clothes, books, and all that stuff but the room itself...? Nope, definitely a parallel universe.

I attempted to lumber out of my pit. My right foot is encased in plaster of Paris, which has been so richly signed with autographs, it looks like a draft version of "Who's Who."

I spied a pair of crutches by my bedside, and after several frustrating attempts to master the art of "stick-walking," I managed to reach the door. I must remember not to direct anyone to "walk this way" today. As I reached for the handle, the door flew open and flattened me to the ground. Mom had charged in and questioned me on what I was doing on the floor. I ignored her question and right away interrogated her to please explain how I ended up like this.

I don't remember a thing! She started blabbing off words like accident, aircraft, parachute, and hospital—all of which did not make any sense to me. At first, I thought I had jumped out of a plane, but she explained to me that I didn't jump—I just happened to be in the wrong place at the wrong time and, in her words, was "landed upon.""

I felt dizzy, trying to make sense of it all. Wow!

What an amazing experience that must have been! I can't wait 'til I remember how I felt.

And so, here I am—commandeering the spare room.

11:00 a.m.

Well, I've had time to recall yesterday's spectacular aerial incident, and so I decided to once again pay a visit to the infamous place, the Northern Districts Annual Medieval Fair. I had hoped that there would be no low-flying, off-course parachuter in the vicinity this time around.

I'm getting used to hobbling around in style, with Bill and Ben, my crutches. I thought I should name them; after all, we're going to be spending a great deal of time together!

I decided to check out the magnificent falconry display. That was a big mistake! I thought they could keep those birds under control! I felt something trickling down my face ... blood!

2:30 P.M.

They're getting to know me quite well here. It's like a home away from home. Even the bed here has my name on it! I'd like to be a doctor when I grow up. I think I'd look really cool, roaming around in a lab coat, sporting a stethoscope.

Half a dozen stitches this time, which I must say is not too bad, considering I could have lost an eye. Lucky Jim. That's what everyone's calling me.

All right, just enough time to get back to the fair to watch the jousting...

LUCKY JIM

Find the answers directly in the text.

1. What event was James attending when he sustained his second injury?

   _____

2. Bill and Ben were James's _____.

3. What was the "mountain of evidence" James refers to in paragraph one?

   _____

4. What happened to cause James's original injury?

   _____

   _____

Think about what the text says.

1. Write three adjectives you think best describe James's personality.

   _____   _____   _____

2. Using examples from the text, explain how you reached this decision.

   _____

   _____

   _____

3. Where was James at 2:30 p.m. on February 28? How do you know?

   _____

   _____

   _____

LUCKY JIM

Applied   Use what you know about the text and your own experience.

1. Why do you think James is now sleeping in the spare room?

_____

_____

_____

_____

2. What might your life be like if you had James's injuries? What would be some of the advantages and disadvantages?

Advantages	**Disadvantages**
_____	_____
_____	_____
_____	_____
_____	_____
_____	_____
_____	_____

3. Write about a time when you, or anyone you know, had an injury that disrupted daily life. How did the injury occur?

_____

_____

_____

_____

_____

LUCKY JIM

Predicting

With reference to the text on page 20, complete the following activity.

1. **a.** What do you think are the chances of James returning home without further incident? Why?

    _____

    _____

    b. Write suggestions for what calamities might befall James at the jousting contest. Include any journeys he might make and the transportation used.

    _____

    _____

    _____

    _____

Making Connections

2. Using your suggestions from question #1, write the entry for James's diary until 6 p.m. Make your entry read as though James has written it.

Genre: Journal

READING FOCUS

- Analyzes and extracts information from a journal to answer literal, inferential, and applied questions
- Makes connections between text and character traits
- Makes predictions about a journal text

ANSWER KEY

Literal (Page 26)

1. Amy sought an investor because, despite her qualifications, she was unable to earn a living as a pilot.

2. Bert Hinkler was an Australian pilot who flew from England to Australia in 15 days.

3. Amy was frightened on the fourth day of her adventure by the sound of what she thought were "desert dogs."

4. Amy crash-landed into a soccer field in Rangoon, India, on the ninth day of her journey. She had to wait three days for repairs, delaying her and making it impossible for her to beat Hinkler's record of 15 days.

5. Amy departed England with only a handful of spectators but returned to a parade of about a million people lining the streets.

Inferential (Page 26)

1. Amy refers to Lord Wakefield as a "believer in dreams" because he financed Amy's dream of owning her own plane.

2. Amy feels second-best when she arrives in Darwin because she did not beat the record of Bert Hinkler in crossing the Atlantic.

3. Countries all over the world were entering World War II.

Applied (Page 27)

1. Answers will vary but should indicate those who didn't believe that women should have pilot's licenses.

2–3. Answers will vary.

Applying Strategies (Page 28)

1–2. Answers will vary.

EXTENSIONS

- Other historical novels students may be interested in reading include the following:
  - *One Came Home* by Amy Timberlake
  - *Countdown* by Deborah Wiles
  - *Navigating Early* by Clare Vanderpool

AMAZING AMY!

Name _____

Read the fictional extracts from the journal of heroic British aviator Amy Johnson, and answer the questions on the following pages.

July 16, 1929: Today is a day for celebration! I have earned my pilot's licence! Let those who tried to dampen my spirit with their doubts and archaic beliefs know that I will fly the sky as their equal, if not their superior!

December 3, 1929: I have come to the conclusion that I must seek out an investor, for I am rich in qualifications—a pilot, a navigator, a ground engineer—yet I can barely afford to feed myself! If I wish to earn a living as a pilot, then I must have my own plane!

May 4, 1930: The day before my grandest adventure! I leave England in the morn—bound for Australia. My savior, Lord Wakefield (rich in oil and a believer in dreams), has given me the capital to purchase a plane. It's a beautiful green Moth that I've named "Jason," after the family business. I shall cross the Atlantic in less than 15 days and beat the record of the Australian Bert Hinkler.

May 8, 1930: My fourth day of flying. I landed in the desert to the frightful sound of desert dogs. With my gun at hand, I waited for them to appear, fearing they might rip me to shreds. Thankfully, no such creature revealed itself to me.

May 11, 1930: Reached Karachi in splendid time! I've traveled 4,000 miles and improved on Hinkler's record by two wonderful days! It amuses me that I left England to only a handful of well-wishers and no journalist to report on my venture (perhaps as they thought it too absurd to be real) and now, I may not only be the first woman to fly solo across the Atlantic, but the first pilot to do so in under 15 days!

May 13, 1930: Nine days in the air, battling monsoon rains and blistering heat, and I've crash-landed my beautiful Moth into a soccer field in Rangoon, India. They say it will be three days before she is in the air again. Impossible!

May 24, 1930: I've journeyed 11,000 miles —an admirable feat, but I feel a failure. The Australians, in Darwin where I landed, have been jolly good sports, calling me a heroic adventurer. Alas, I don't feel heroic. I feel weary and second-best.

The Daily Mail (who thought my departure was not newsworthy) is awarding me 10,000 pounds for such a daring feat! They say a telegram from the King and Queen should also be expected!

July 1930: It has been one year since I earned my pilot's licence. Today I was driven through the streets of London in a parade so that one million English fans could welcome me home!

July 1932: London to Cape Town in 11 hours! I have finally broken a record! Now I must plan my next adventure. I think England to New York!

January 4, 1941: The whole world has changed! We continue to ferry pilots and aircrafts from the factories to the RAF bases. At least I am contributing to the war effort. The weather has been disastrous of late! Thick fog and freezing. I head off again tomorrow.

AMAZING AMY!

Literal   Find the answers directly in the text.

1. What factors prompted Amy to seek out an investor to finance a plane?

   _____

   _____

2. Who is Bert Hinkler? _____

   _____

3. What frightens Amy on May 8, 1930? _____

   _____

4. What event delays Amy's attempt at the record? _____

   _____

5. How does Amy's departure from England compare to her return? _____

   _____

   _____

Inferential   Think about what the text says.

1. Why does Amy refer to Lord Wakefield as a "believer in dreams"?

   _____

   _____

2. Why does Amy feel second-best when she arrives in Darwin?

   _____

   _____

3. What do you think Amy means by the remark that the "whole world has changed" in her final entry?

   _____

   _____

AMAZING AMY!

Applied   Use what you know about the text and your own experience.

1. Who do you think tried to dampen Amy's spirit with "their doubts and archaic beliefs"?

   _____

   _____

   _____

2. Amy Johnson is known as Britain's most famous pilot. Why do you think she earned so much fame?

   _____

   _____

   _____

   _____

3. Write about a time when you felt as though you were second-best.

   _____

   _____

   _____

   _____

   _____

   _____

   _____

   _____

   _____

   _____

   _____

AMAZING AMY!

Predicting

Use the text on page 25 to complete the following activities and make some predictions.

1. **a.** When you read the text about aviator Amy Johnson, what questions come to mind about her and her life? Discuss your thoughts with a partner, and record a few questions on the lines below.

    _____

    _____

    _____

    _____

    b. Join with another pair of students and discuss possible answers to your questions. Circle one of the questions above and write the answer that your group agreed upon below.

    _____

    _____

    _____

2. Imagine that the journal entry dated January 4, 1941 was Amy Johnson's last entry. What happened to her? Create the *Daily Mail*'s front page article that explains why it was Amy's final entry in her journal. Include some information about Amy's achievements and the type of person she was. Create a short headline that will grab readers' attention. Include a drawing you think matches the story.

Daily Mail   January 6, 1941

_____   _____

_____   _____

_____   _____

_____   [   ]   _____

_____   [   ]   _____

_____   [   ]   _____

_____   [   ]   _____

_____   [   ]   _____

_____   _____

Genre: Myth

READING FOCUS

- Analyzes and extracts information from a myth to answer literal, inferential, and applied questions
- Makes connections between text and character traits
- Compares similarities and differences between his/her rating for a character in a text and the rating given by other classmates

ANSWER KEY

Literal (Page 31)

1. Four of the following: handsome child; beautiful clothes; attractive ornaments; long, dark hair; tightly coiled hair; peacock feather in hair

2. Four of the following: fish, wading birds, crocodiles, forest trees, any person or animal that drank from the river.

Inferential (Page 31)

1. a. contaminated (5)   b. treacherous (6)

   c. purposefully (6)   d. merciful (8)

   e. exhilarated (9)   f. pleaded (8)

   g. banished (8)   h. wistful (4)

   i. lilting (3)   j. revered (1)

2. "Even the wild jungle animals quieted down at the sound of his flute."
   "Krishna was able to hold his breath for as long as he wanted."

Applied (Page 32)

1–3. Answers will vary.

Applying Strategies (Page 33)

Answers will vary.

EXTENSIONS

- Students who would enjoy reading other Indian myths can visit the following website: *http://www.indianmythology.com/finish.*
- Students can read myths from other countries on the following website: *http://www.myths.e2bn.org/mythsandlegends.*

Name _____

Read the myth and answer the questions on the following pages.

Lord Krishna is one of the most revered deities (gods) in the Hindu faith, and there are numerous myths involving him, many of which depict him destroying evil powers. The story of Krishna and the serpent Kaliyan is very well known. It is set near the Yamuna River, which, along with the Ganges, is one of the most sacred rivers in India.

Krishna lived in a village near the Yamuna River. He was a handsome child who always wore beautiful clothes adorned with attractive ornaments. Krishna's long, dark hair was coiled tightly around top of his head and tied in a knot, into which he often placed a peacock's feather.

Krishna was a charming child and liked by everyone—even when he was yet again found playing pranks on people. He delighted in listening to and playing music and was an excellent flutist. Whenever he played his flute, everyone would stop what they were doing to come and listen to his lilting tunes. Even the wild jungle animals quieted down at the sound of his flute.

Krishna's job was to help take the cattle into the jungle near the river every morning and bring them home in the evening. Here, plenty of grass was available for the cattle to graze on and water to drink. One day, as Krishna was playing a wistful tune to the other cowherds, a huge, poisonous serpent named Kaliyan slithered past them and into the river. He had decided to make his new home in the deepest part.

Soon, however, the river became contaminated by Kaliyan's poison. Any person or animal that drank from the river perished. Poisoned fish, wading birds, and crocodiles floated upside down in the water. Even the forest trees on the river bank shriveled up and died. The river had been the source of fresh water for all living things surrounding the area, and great suffering was endured by all.

Krishna decided to teach the treacherous serpent a lesson. He walked purposefully up to the river bank, jumped in at the deepest part, and swam to Kaliyan's home. Kaliyan immediately launched himself at Krishna to crush him to death. But Krishna was too quick and swam to the surface, followed by Kaliyan. In an instant, Krishna got hold of Kaliyan's head and stood on it. Kaliyan tried in vain to shake him off. He dove deep into the water with Krishna still secured firmly on his head. Kaliyan's plan was to try to drown Krishna, but Krishna was able to hold his breath for as long as he wanted. Kaliyan was forced to swim back to the surface for air.

Throngs of terrified villagers gathered on the river bank to witness Krishna's struggle with the hated serpent. Kaliyan tried to twist around to bite Krishna, who managed to get both his hands around the serpent's head. He began kicking the snake as hard as he could. Slowly but surely, Kaliyan began to weaken, as he could not withstand the pain of Krishna's assault. He started spurting venom, but Krishna continued to attack him until all the venom had come out.

Finally, the huge serpent gave up the struggle and pleaded with Krishna to spare his life. Krishna heard his plea and decided to be merciful. He banished Kaliyan from the Yamuna. Kaliyan slithered painfully away, never to be seen again.

The exhilarated villagers cheered Krishna as he swam ashore. Thanks to his almighty feat, the river was pure once more.

Name _____

KRISHNA AND THE SERPENT

Literal   Find the answers directly in the text.

1. From the second paragraph, list four separate phrases that describe Krishna's appearance.

    • _____

    • _____

    • _____

    • _____

2. List four living things that perished after being poisoned by Kaliyan.

    • _____

    • _____

    • _____

    • _____

Inferential   Think about what the text says.

1. Write a synonym from the text for each word below, and in the box, write the number of the paragraph it is found in.

   a. polluted _____ ☐   **b.** dangerous _____ ☐

   c. determinedly _____ ☐   **d.** forgiving _____ ☐

   e. delighted _____ ☐   **f.** begged _____ ☐

   g. banned _____ ☐   **h.** thoughtful _____ ☐

   i. rhythmical _____ ☐   **j.** honored _____ ☐

2. There is evidence in the story to suggest Krishna possessed special powers. Give two examples of this.

    • _____

    • _____

KRISHNA AND THE SERPENT

Applied   Use what you know about the text and your own experience.

1. Do you think Kaliyan deserved Krishna's mercy? Explain your answer in detail.

   _____

   _____

   _____

   _____

   _____

   _____

2. How else could Krishna have taught the serpent a lesson?

   _____

   _____

   _____

   _____

3. Krishna improved the quality of life for the villagers by banishing Kaliyan from the Yamuna. In what ways do you think life changed for the villagers?

   _____

   _____

   _____

   _____

   _____

   _____

   _____

KRISHNA AND THE SERPENT

Use the text on page 30 to complete the character ratings for Krishna and Kaliyan. Then, compare your answers with those of other classmates. Write a comment for each character's rating.

Krishna's Character Rating

	Extremely	A Bit	Uncertain	A Bit	Extremely	
Kind						**Cruel**
Comment:						
Fearless						**Cowardly**
Comment:						
Friendly						**Unfriendly**
Comment:						
Strong-Willed						**Weak-Willed**
Comment:						
Generous						**Selfish**
Comment:						

Kaliyan's Character Rating

	Extremely	A Bit	Uncertain	A Bit	Extremely	
Kind						**Cruel**
Comment:						
Fearless						**Cowardly**
Comment:						
Friendly						**Unfriendly**
Comment:						
Strong-Willed						**Weak-Willed**
Comment:						
Generous						**Selfish**
Comment						

Genre: Folktale

READING FOCUS

- Analyzes and extracts information from a folktale to answer literal, inferential, and applied questions
- Determines the sequence of events within the text
- Makes connections between characters to create a family tree

---

ANSWER KEY

Literal (Page 36)

1. the Lake of the Red Eye, the Sea of Moyle, the land of Erris
2. Lairgnen, the man from the north, and Doech, the woman from the south
3. The children kept their voices and could sing beautifully.

Inferential (Page 36)

1. Answers will vary. Possible answer(s): unhappy, miserable, dismal, destroyed.
2. a–d. Answers will vary.

Applied (Page 37)

1. It was in honor of the children.
2. a–b. Answers will vary.
3.

Lake of the Red Eye		Land of Erris	
1–300 years	300–600 years	600–900 years	End of Life
	Sea of Moyle		Hill of the White Field

Applying Strategies (Page 38)

1. Placement of events will vary but should be in the following chronological order:
   - King Dearg elected as chieftain
   - Lir and Ove wed
   - children born
   - Ove perishes
   - Lir and Oifa marry
   - children turned into swans
   - Oifa turned into an air demon
   - decree that no swans be harmed
   - swans at the Lake of Red Eye
   - swans in the Sea of Moyle
   - swans in the land of Erris
   - swans return home
   - swans revert to human form
   - children perish

2. a.

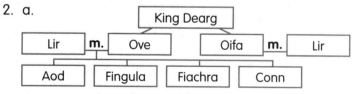

b. Grandfather (grandparent)

c. Stepmother and aunt

EXTENSIONS

- Teachers can suggest the following to students:
  - research other Celtic folktales from Ireland, Wales, Scotland, Cornwall in England, and Brittany in France.
  - locate real places mentioned in tales on a map of the abovementioned Celtic regions.
  - research Celtic place names (e.g., Erin and Albain are the Celtic names for Ireland and Scotland).

THE CHILDREN OF LIR

Name _____

Read the Irish folktale and answer the questions on the following pages.

The five kings of Erin met to decide who would become overall king of the isle. King Lir of the Hill of the White Field expected to be elected. When King Dearg was chosen, Lir was incensed, and he returned home feeling great outrage. The other three wanted to attack Lir for his refusal to acknowledge Dearg as chieftain. Dearg restrained them, requesting that their lives remain peaceful.

To pacify Lir, Dearg offered him the hand of his eldest daughter, Ove. Lir and Ove were very happy and were soon blessed with twins—a son, Aod, and a daughter, Fingula. A while later, the twin sons Fiachra and Conn were born. Sadly, Ove did not live long enough to hold them in her arms or even to lay her motherly eyes upon them.

Lir mourned bitterly for his beloved wife, and had it not been for his children whom he loved dearly, he would have died of grief. In time, Lir married Ove's sister, Oifa, who was full of love and affection for Lir and his four children. But as Lir's love for his children grew deeper than his love for her, Oifa grew jealous and bitter. Soon, her feelings for the children of Lir were those of hatred and simmering rage.

One day, Oifa took the children to the Lake of the Red Eye. As they were bathing in the cool, clear waters, she cast a spell and turned them into four beautiful white swans.

"Like this you will stay for 900 years, until Lairgnen, the man from the north, marries Deoch, the woman from the south. But I will grant you two things—you will retain your voices and your songs will be the sweetest-sounding arias ever heard."

Lir knew that Oifa had somehow harmed his children. He set off toward the lake, where he was confronted with the reality of Oifa's cruel work. He was distraught. As he bade his children farewell, he knew his life would never again know happiness.

When King Dearg heard of Oifa's malicious deed, he used his Druid wand for spells and sorcery against her, compelling her to spend eternity in a life of misery as an air demon.

The people were so sadly grieved at the loss of the children that it was decreed that no swan would ever again be harmed on the isle of Erin.

For 300 years, the children of Lir spent their time on the Lake of the Red Eye, captivating everyone with their enchanting songs. Eventually, the time came for the swans to fly to the open Sea of Moyle between Erin and Albain. Here they would spend 300 years in cold and misery, ravaged by hunger and violent storms. The swans endured another 300 miserable years in the desolate land of Erris, before returning home to the Hill of the White Field. But how everything had changed! Ruins and overgrown gardens were all that was left of their once charming home—just bleak desolation and decay.

At this time, Lairgnen, prince of the north, was to marry Deoch, daughter of the king of the south. She had heard of the magnificent swans with their beautiful singing voices. She refused to marry Lairgnen until he captured them for her as a wedding present. Lairgnen was close to achieving this goal, but as he touched the wings of the birds, they lost their feathers and transformed back to their human forms. But time had not stood still for them, no longer were they young children full of life and joy, but four wizened and withered old folk, ready for the grave.

The four were buried together, and a cairn was raised for them. Such was the fate of the children of Lir.

To this day, no one is allowed to harm a swan in Ireland, the land of Erin.

Activities

THE CHILDREN OF LIR

Literal   Find the answers directly in the text.

1. List the places the swans spent each 300-year period.

   _____

   _____

2. According to the curse, before the swans could be released, who had to be married?

   _____

   _____

3. What parting gifts did Oifa leave with the children of Lir?

   _____

   _____

Inferential   Think about what the text says.

1. How do you think the children felt when they returned home to the Hill of the White Field? Explain your answer.

   _____

   _____

   _____

   _____

2. Read each sentence. Decide if each statement is **True** or **False**.

   a. Lir was happy that Dearg was   ☐ True ☐ False
      chosen as chieftain.

   b. Lir was a doting father.   ☐ True ☐ False

   c. The children enjoyed their time   ☐ True ☐ False
      as swans.

   d. Dearg was a righteous king.   ☐ True ☐ False

THE CHILDREN OF LIR

Applied   Use what you know about the text and your own experience.

1. Why do you think it was decreed that no swans should be harmed on the isle of Erin?

_____

_____

_____

2. **a.** Choose a character from this sad folktale.

   ☐ King Lir   ☐ King Dearg   ☐ Oifa   ☐ the children of Lir

   b. Explain why your chosen character was unhappy.

   _____

   _____

   _____

   _____

   _____

3. Compete the timeline for the 900 years that the children of Lir were swans. Label each section of the timeline and the places where the swans were for each section.

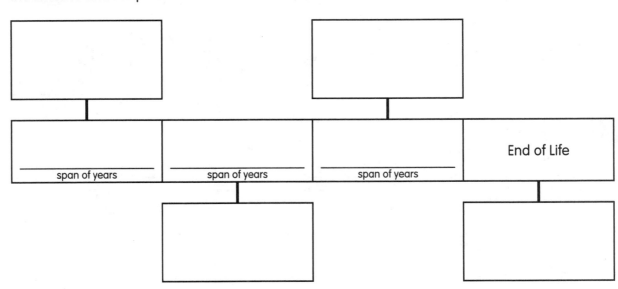

THE CHILDREN OF LIR

Sequencing

Refer to the folktale on page 35 and sequence the events that take place in the story.

1. The story naturally falls into four parts. Consider where you think the divisions occur, and in chronological order, place these events in the correct boxes.

- Lir and Oifa marry
- swans in the Sea of Moyle
- swans revert to human form
- Oifa turned into an air demon
- swans return home

- children turned into swans
- decree that no swans be harmed
- King Dearg elected as chieftain
- swans in the land of Erris
- swans at the Lake of Red Eye

- Ove perishes
- children perish
- Lir and Ove wed
- children born

Part One	Part Two
_____	_____
_____	_____
_____	_____
_____	_____
Part Three	**Part Four**
_____	_____
_____	_____
_____	_____
_____	_____

2. **a.** Complete the family tree for the children of Lir.

Making Connections

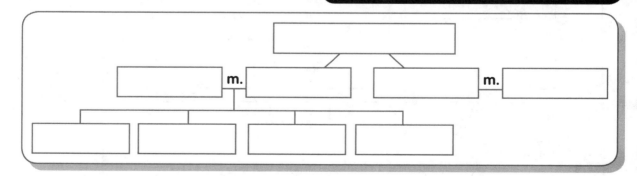

b. What relation is King Dearg to the children of Lir?

_____

c. What two categories of relationship does Oifa have with the children?

_____

Genre: Mystery

READING FOCUS

- Analyzes and extracts information from a mystery to answer literal, inferential, and applied questions
- Makes connections between a text and the conventions of the mystery genre to plot a chapter

ANSWER KEY

Literal (Page 41)

1. a. False   b. True   c. False   d. True

2. She wants to see if there is anything behind the tapestry.

Inferential (Page 41)

1. She is worried he might have seen her watching him.

2. Answers will vary. Possible answer(s): mysterious, secretive, serious.

Applied (Page 42)

1–2. Answers will vary.

Applying Strategies (Page 43)

1. Answers will vary. Possible answer(s): a problem or puzzle to solve, something that is missing, a secret, an event that is not explained.

2–3. Answers will vary.

EXTENSIONS

- Other mystery titles students may enjoy reading include the following:
  - *Antonio S and the Mystery of Theodore Guzman* by Odo Hirsch
  - *Emily Eyefinger* series by Duncan Ball
  - *Encyclopedia Brown* series by Donald J. Sobol
  - *The Roman Mysteries* series by Caroline Lawrence

THE MYSTERY OF THE LOCKED DOOR

Name _____

Read the chapter from a mystery novel and answer the questions on the following pages.

Chapter 6

Kate held her breath as she watched her uncle carefully place the key inside the photo frame. So that's where he kept it. She couldn't believe it had taken two weeks of her vacation with her aunt and uncle to find out. Kate ducked back around the corner and hoped he hadn't seen her.

"Kate?"

Her heart pounding, she walked into the room. "Yes, Uncle Stanley?"

"I'm going out for a walk. You stay here and don't get into any trouble. Your aunt will be back any minute now."

"Okay." She tried not to look too excited.

He glared at her for a few seconds, tapped his cane, and stalked toward the front door.

As soon as Kate heard the door slam, she headed for the fireplace and retrieved the key from inside the photo frame. Finally, she was going to find out why Uncle Stanley always locked the door to the attic. She turned and raced up the stairs, reaching the door within seconds. Her hands shook as she fitted the key into the lock. Kate paused for a moment, then pushed open the door. It was dark inside, and she felt for the light switch. She flicked it on and took in the scene in front of her.

The room was filled with all kinds of junk—stacks of boxes, neglected wooden furniture, and piles of clothing. It smelled musty, making Kate feel queasy. Trying to ignore it, she looked around. Why had her uncle gone to so much trouble to keep her out of here? What was his secret? Kate's eyes fell on a small table near the far wall. She could see a handprint in the thick layer of dust on the table. She walked over and examined it. Someone must have been here recently.

Her glance wandered up to the wall behind the table. The mournful eyes of a woman gazed at her from a moldy tapestry.

Kate shivered. "What's going on?" she whispered.

She knew it was silly to talk to a tapestry, but she felt as though this woman was hiding a secret. Was she? A thought struck her. Could there be something behind the tapestry?

Kate carefully squeezed into the gap between the table and the wall. Then she reached out and moved the tapestry to one side. She gasped.

Name _____

THE MYSTERY OF THE LOCKED DOOR

Literal   Find the answers directly in the text.

1. Read each sentence. Decide if each statement is **True** or **False**.

   a. Kate felt queasy because she was frightened.   ☐ True ☐ False

   b. Uncle Stanley had hidden the key to the attic.   ☐ True ☐ False

   c. Kate knew someone had been near the table
   because it had been cleaned.   ☐ True ☐ False

   d. Kate was in a hurry to get to the attic.   ☐ True ☐ False

2. Why does Kate squeeze into the gap between the wall and the table?

   _____

   _____

   _____

Inferential   Think about what the text says.

1. Why do you think Kate's heart was pounding when she went to talk to Uncle Stanley?

   _____

   _____

2. List words or phrases that describe Uncle Stanley.

   _____

   _____

   _____

THE MYSTERY OF THE LOCKED DOOR

Applied   Use what you know about the text and your own experience.

1. Imagine Uncle Stanley sneaks back into the house and catches Kate as she is running up the stairs. Write what you think they would say to each other.

Uncle Stanley: _____

_____

_____

Kate: _____

_____

_____

Uncle Stanley: _____

_____

_____

Kate: _____

_____

_____

2. The chapter is written from Kate's point of view. Write it instead from the point of view of the mournful-eyed woman in the tapestry. Below, begin with her hearing Kate run up the stairs. You may finish on a separate sheet of paper.

_____

_____

_____

_____

_____

_____

_____

_____

Name _____

THE MYSTERY OF THE LOCKED DOOR

Mystery novels are full of mysterious or puzzling elements.

1. List some more examples of mysterious or puzzling elements a mystery novel might use.

secret codes, the disappearance of someone, a locked room, _____

_____

2. Use your ideas to help you plan the next chapter of *The Mystery of the Locked Door*. To begin, write two possibilities for what Kate might find behind the tapestry. Circle the one you like better, then continue the process down the page. Part of Chapter 6 has been done as an example.

Kate Sees Uncle Stanley Hide the Key

What happens next?	Kate follows Uncle Stanley	OR	Kate steals the key
What happens next?	Kate finds	OR	Kate finds
What happens next?		OR	
What happens next?		OR	
What happens next?		OR	
What happens next?		OR	

How do you want your chapter to end? To keep a reader turning pages, mystery novel chapters often end on a note of suspense.

3. List some suspenseful ways a mystery novel chapter might end.

_____

_____

_____

Genre: Adventure

READING FOCUS

- Analyzes and extracts information from an adventure story to answer literal, inferential, and applied questions
- Uses sensory imaging to set the scene for the reader
- Predicts and makes connections between the text and its characters' traits

---

ANSWER KEY

Literal (Page 46)

1. False 2. True 3. True 4. False

Inferential (Page 46)

1. The three boys were carrying too much stuff with them, and it would've been a slow ride.

2. The boys are taking the lamb and the ewe back to the farm to put them into a small pen so that the lamb can get close to the ewe to feed.

3. The small crayfish are put back into the dam to give them a chance to grow larger.

Applied (Page 47)

1–3. Answers will vary.

Applying Strategies (Page 48)

1–2. Answers will vary.

EXTENSIONS

- Other adventure stories include the following:
  - *Alanna: The First Adventure* by Tamora Pierce
  - *The Dark Is Rising* by Susan Cooper
  - *Wonderstruck* by Brian Seiznick

THE RESCUE

Name _____

Read the adventure story and answer the questions on the following pages.

Colin knows he's showing off, but he doesn't care. He rides around the fuel pump stations, does a donut on the grass, and skids dangerously close to a heap of rusting scrap metal, which is the graveyard for the farm's old vehicles. He skids to a halt by the two boys who are leaning against their own motorbikes, covering them with red dust. Colin removes his helmet and grins at his two best buddies.

"'Bout time you guys got here! Let's go in. Mom's making us some lunch to take with us." The boys follow the waft of bacon over to the house and collect their lunch from Mrs. Bell. They fill up their water bottles, and each grabs a crayfish net from the shed. As they walk back to the bikes, Simon notices that Colin's motorbike is on a slant.

"Hey, Colin! Think you might have a flat!"

Colin curses under his breath.

"Dumb junk metal! There's a giant gash in my tire!" he declares angrily.

"I could give you a ride on my bike, but with our backpacks and the nets, it'll be a slow trip," suggests Shane.

Simon has an idea. After some persuasion, Colin agrees to take Mr. Bell's old truck from the shed but only if Shane drives. As his dad lets him drive around the farm on weekends, Shane excitedly agrees. The boys throw the crayfish nets into the back of the truck and drive away from the house. The sound of the truck leaving alerts the sheepdogs, who bark their farewell.

The first dam the boys arrive at is nearly empty. Dead crayfish are floating on top of the mud, and the ducks are enjoying a mid-morning feast.

"Phew! This dam stinks!" Shane remarks, putting the truck into reverse. The boys drive along the fence road to the next dam, which is completely dry.

"Rain better come soon," Simon mutters. The other boys nod in silence, contemplating the consequences of another bad season.

Pulling up at the lip of the third dam, the truck scares a flock of sheep from their drinking hole. The boys cheer as they see it's full of fresh water. The nets are collected, and slimy chunks of raw meat are skewered onto the metal hooks. Each boy drops a net into the murky, brown water of the dam. They sit on its banks and begin digging around in their backpacks for their sandwiches.

With his mouth full of homemade bread, bacon, and runny egg, Simon realizes he can hear a strange noise. "Woz dat 'oise?" he asks, his words muffled. A panicked cry echoes across the field.

Colin jumps up and walks over the other side of the dam. "Look at this! I think she's in trouble! Shane, grab that old shirt from under the seat in the truck." One of Colin's dad's prized ewes is on its side, the back legs of a tiny lamb jutting out from behind it.

"It's definitely stuck!" Colin takes the shirt from Shane and places it around the tiny back legs of the lamb. With a gentle pull from Colin, the lamb is out, spluttering and bleating. Colin takes the lamb around for its mother to smell and get its scent. The ewe isn't interested.

"Can you two lift the ewe onto the back of the truck?" asks Colin, carrying the lamb toward the dam. "We can put them into a small pen in the sheep yards at home. She'll have to let the lamb near her then."

With the ewe and its lamb securely on the back of the truck, the boys walk over to where they dropped the nets.

"Okay. Let's pull them in!" The boys carefully drag the nets onto the dam's bank and find them overflowing with crayfish. They tip them out onto the bank, chasing the escapees who shuffle backwards to the water. The boys sort the crayfish—big ones in the buckets, smaller ones go back in the dam for now. With their buckets full to the brim, they carry them to the truck.

"Heh, Colin. I think your dad's gonna realize we took his truck when we show up with the ewe and the lamb," remarks Simon, watching the lamb trying unsuccessfully to get a drink from its mother. "At least we saved the lamb, right?"

"And we've got three buckets of crayfish for dinner!" offers Shane.

Colin climbs into the front of the truck, thinking.

"Well . . . we're about to find out!"

THE RESCUE

Literal   Find the answers directly in the text.

Read each sentence. Decide if each statement is **True** or **False**.

1. Shane is chosen to drive the truck as he is the biggest and can reach the pedals.   ☐ True   ☐ False

2. The second dam the boys go to is completely dry.   ☐ True   ☐ False

3. Raw meat is used to bait the nets to catch the crayfish.   ☐ True   ☐ False

4. The larger crayfish are thrown back into the dam.   ☐ True   ☐ False

Inferential   Think about what the text says.

1. Why don't the boys take the two motorbikes to the dam?

_____

_____

_____

2. Why are the boys taking the ewe and the lamb back to the farm?

_____

_____

_____

3. Why are the larger crayfish taken and the smaller ones put back into the dam?

_____

_____

_____

THE RESCUE

Applied   Use what you know about the text and your own experience.

1. How old do you think the boys are? _____

2. What type of character do you think Colin is?

   _____

   _____

   _____

   _____

   _____

3. "Rain better come soon," Simon mutters. The other boys nod in silence, contemplating the consequences of another bad season.

   What do these two sentences tell us about life on a farm? Make some notes below.

   _____

   _____

   _____

   _____

   _____

   _____

   _____

   _____

   _____

   _____

   _____

THE RESCUE

Answer these questions about the text from page 45. To help readers imagine a clear picture of a setting in a story, authors often use the five senses to describe the scene. This can help readers enjoy the story, especially if the setting is a place unfamiliar to them, such as a farm.

1. **a.** Reread the story. Highlight the sentences or phrases that use one of the senses to describe the scene. In bullet-point form, record your findings in the boxes below.

What Did the Boys See?	What Did the Boys Hear?	What Did They Smell?
What Did They Touch?		**What Did They Taste?**

b. Did you have a clear picture of the boys on the farm when you read the story? In your answer, include what helped you to make connections to the text (e.g., the senses described, having visited a farm before, or having read other stories similar to this one).

_____

_____

_____

_____

2. What happens when the boys arrive back at the house? Finish the story by writing the final paragraph. Include dialogue between the boys and Mr. Bell.

Predicting

_____

_____

_____

_____

Genre: Suspense

READING FOCUS

- Analyzes and extracts information from a suspense/ supernatural narrative to answer literal, inferential, and applied questions
- Makes comparisons and connections from the text to create character profiles
- Determines important information to analyze key elements of a story

ANSWER KEY

Literal (Page 51)

1. he wanted to help his father with the garden.
2. Ben poured purple stuff into the class fish tank.
3. His eyes were almost colorless.

Inferential (Page 51)

1. Ben had a bad feeling about his detention because something strange had happened to his friends after their detention.
2. Jake looked and acted differently.
3. Answers should indicate that they were distracted students, often got into trouble, and didn't apply themselves.

Applied (Page 52)

1. He will change just like his friends did.
2. The story leaves you with uncertainty as to what will happen to Ben.
3.

Genre—Suspense		Title—"The Wizard"
Evaluative Comment About Title—Answers will vary.		
Characters—Ben, Mr. Wizard, Jake, and Alex		Setting—School
Events and Action—The boys decided to put the new teacher to the test, which led to Jake getting detention. At detention, Mr. Wizard offered him a drink and cookies. Ben asked Jake to go to the river, but Jake decided to help his dad instead. Ben went down to the river with Alex instead. At school, Ben noticed that Jake had changed. Alex received detention next for not doing his homework. The next day, Alex seemed different as well. Then, Ben put purple stuff into the fish tank, which got him detention. The story ends with Ben having one of Mr. Wizard's cookies.		

Applying Strategies (Page 53)

Answers will vary.

EXTENSIONS

- Students can compile lists of authors of the suspense/supernatural genre and titles.
- Brainstorm the different characteristics and features of this genre.
- Discuss the effectiveness of leaving "what happens next" to the readers' imagination.

Name _____

Read the suspense narrative and answer the questions on the following pages.

You should see this new teacher at our school. He's old with thick gray hair, and he wears an immaculate suit and tie. His pants have a crease down the front that is so sharp it could cut butter, and his shoes shine so brightly we need sunglasses for the glare. We decided it was time to put the new teacher to the test. But despite our best efforts, he stayed calm, cool, and collected. He ignored most of what we did until my friend Jake spilled some stuff all over the kid who sits in front of him. Mr. Wizard stared at him with his strange, almost colorless eyes and suggested that they should have a meeting after school. A detention on day one—that must be a record, even for Jake!

I called Jake to see how it all went. Jake sounded a bit subdued and different. He just said that the old guy had talked to him for a while, offered him a drink and some cookies, and sent him home. Going down to the river to mess around as we often do seemed like a good idea, but when I suggested it, Jake said something about wanting to help his dad with the garden. That's a joke! He must have something really special planned. I can't wait to hear about it tomorrow. I called Alex, and we wandered down to the river where we threw some rocks into the water and onto some roofs until a mean, ugly dog started to make a racket, and we decided we'd better get out of there.

I just can't understand it. Jake arrived at school the next day with his shirt tucked in, his hair combed, and he actually worked hard. He spoke politely, offered to do boring jobs, and he'd even done his homework! He must be sick. Alex had scribbled "homework stinks" all over his paper, because like me, he didn't have time to look at it. I got away with it, but he got a detention. I don't think Mr. Wizard has a home; he seems to be here all the time. He's not like any teacher I've ever had before.

Alex got a ridiculously high grade on his homework the following day, and he really looked like he cared. He seemed different. I'm not sure what it was, but the fun-loving, into-anything friend I had been in so much trouble with had disappeared. It's scary. He and Jake were talking about joining the Boy Scouts so they could do some community service. I felt as if they were strangers. I didn't understand what had changed.

The next day, I had to go to detention after school! All I did was add some purple stuff into the class fish tank. The fish are a bit lethargic but still alive. I thought it looked cool, but Mr. Wizard didn't agree. Boy, are his eyes strange! So in I walked, with a really bad feeling in the pit of my stomach, and he sat me down and said:

"Ben, I've been really looking forward to having this chat with you. Would you like a drink and some of my homemade cookies?"

He poured me some green drink and handed me a cookie that tasted like nothing I had ever eaten before, and we started to talk.

THE WIZARD

Literal   Find the answers directly in the text.

1. Jake wouldn't go down to the river because _____

_____.

2. What did Ben do to get a detention?

_____

_____

3. What was strange about Mr. Wizard's eyes?

_____

Inferential   Think about what the text says.

1. Why did Ben have a bad feeling about his detention?

_____

_____

2. How did Ben know that Jake had changed?

_____

_____

3. What kind of students were the boys prior to detention?

_____

_____

_____

THE WIZARD

Applied   Use what you know about the text and your own experience.

1. Most likely, what might happen to Ben?

_____

_____

2. Explain why this narrative is classified as a suspense story.

_____

_____

3. Analyze the key elements of the story by completing the diagram.

Genre	Title
Evaluative Comment About Title	
Characters	**Setting**
Events and Action	

Name _____

THE WIZARD

Complete these two profiles of Mr. Wizard. The first one is a self-profile, and the second is one that Ben may have made about his teacher. You will need to use what you were told about Mr. Wizard and the assumptions you made from the text on page 50. Compare the finished profiles.

Self-Profile—Geoffrey Wizard
Appearance
Personality

Likes	Dislikes

Wishes

My Teacher—Mr. Wizard
Appearance
Personality

Likes	Dislikes

Wishes

School Timetable

Genre: Informational Text—Timetable

READING FOCUS

- Analyzes and extracts information from a school timetable to answer literal, inferential, and applied questions
- Makes connections and compares timetable information with own experiences
- Formulates literal, inferential, and applied questions

ANSWER KEY

Literal (Page 56)

1. b
2. c
3. Spanish
4. Friday
5. Monday
6. one day

Inferential (Page 56)

1. Tuesday
2. Language Arts; an hour and a half, five days a week is dedicated to Language Arts

Applied (Page 57)

1–3. Answers will vary.

Applying Strategies (Page 58)

1–2. Answers will vary.

EXTENSIONS

- Collect examples of different timetables and list similarities and differences.
- Students can write descriptive text to provide the same information given in a section of a timetable and compare the two in terms of ease of use and presentation time.

SCHOOL TIMETABLE

Name _____

Read the school timetable and answer the questions on the following pages.

School Timetable

Time	Monday	Tuesday	Wednesday	Thursday	Friday
8:45–9:00	Daily Fitness	Daily Fitness	Daily Fitness	Daily Fitness	School Assembly
9:00–9:45	Language Arts	Language Arts	Language Arts	Language Arts	Language Arts
9:45–10:30	Language Arts	Language Arts	Language Arts	Language Arts	Language Arts
			Recess		
10:45–11:30	Mathematics	Mathematics	Mathematics	Mathematics	Mathematics
11:30–12:15	Library	Spanish	Mathematics	Health	Music
			Lunch		
12:55–1:40	Social Studies	Science	Social Studies	Science	Social Studies
1:40–2:25	Social Studies	Science	Art	Drama	Physical Education
2:25–3:15	Health	Health	Art	Drama	Physical Education

SCHOOL TIMETABLE

Literal   Find the answers directly in the text.

1. On Thursday, the time spent on science is . . .

   a. ☐ the same as on Tuesday.

   b. ☐ more than on Monday.

   c. ☐ less than on Friday.

   d. ☐ the same as on Wednesday.

2. The class has a mathematics lesson . . .

   a. ☐ before recess.

   b. ☐ after Spanish on Tuesday.

   c. ☐ every day.

   d. ☐ for two periods on Friday.

3. Which language (other than English) does this class study? _____

4. On which day does this class have physical education? _____

5. What day do the students need to make sure they have their library books to turn in?

   _____

6. How many days a week does the class have music? _____

Inferential   Think about what the text says.

1. On which day would this class be most likely to do a science experiment?

   _____

   _____

2. Which subject do you think the teacher considers to be the most important? Explain why you think this.

   _____

   _____

   _____

   _____

SCHOOL TIMETABLE

Applied   Use what you know about the text and your own experience.

1. **a.** On which day(s) does *your* class have physical education? _____

    b. Which day do you think is the best day to have physical education? _____

    c. Give reasons. _____

    _____

    _____

2. **a.** From the timetable, which day would you like the most? _____

    b. Explain why. _____

    _____

    _____

3. **a.** Give three reasons why a teacher would make up a class timetable.

    * _____

    _____

    * _____

    _____

    * _____

    _____

    b. List other types of timetables.

    _____

    _____

    _____

    _____

    _____

    _____

SCHOOL TIMETABLE

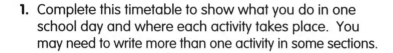

Making Connections

1. Complete this timetable to show what you do in one school day and where each activity takes place. You may need to write more than one activity in some sections.

Time	Activities	Location
5:00 a.m. to 6:00		
6:00 to 7:00		
7:00 to 8:00		
8:00 to 9:00		
9:00 to 10:00		
10:00 to 11:00		
11:00 to noon		
noon to 1:00 p.m.		
1:00 to 2:00		
2:00 to 3:00		
3:00 to 4:00		
4:00 to 5:00		
5:00 to 6:00		
6:00 to 7:00		
7:00 to 8:00		

2. Timetables should make information more readily available to the reader.

a. Use the information provided in your timetable in order to write five questions for another student to answer. Try to make your questions challenging so that the reader has to read, think, and interpret some of your information.

- _____
  _____
- _____
  _____
- _____
  _____
- _____
  _____
- _____
  _____

b. Which question do you think is the most challenging and why?

_____
_____
_____
_____
_____
_____
_____

Genre: Letter

Teacher Information

READING FOCUS

- Analyzes and extracts information from two letters to answer literal, inferential, and applied questions
- Makes comparisons between the two texts
- Makes connections between text and character traits

ANSWER KEY

Literal (Page 61)

1. Yes	2. Yes	3. No	4. Yes	5. No	6. Yes

Inferential (Page 61)

1. Kathy discovered her mom's clothes still hanging and her belongings still sitting on her dresser just as she had left them. It's hard to face that her mom is no longer with them.

2. The pond meant a lot to his wife and to him.

3. The trip is to take care of loose ends with the passing of Kathy's mom.

Applied (Page 62)

1–4. Answers will vary.

Applying Strategies (Page 63)

1.

Event	Max	Kathy
Seeing Granddad's house	thinks the house is skinny and is glad that his own house isn't joined to another house	noticed the changes; hedges are overgrown and front garden needs weeding
Seeing Granddad	observed that Granddad likes wearing ties and smells like soap, interested in Granddad's stamp collection	observed that her dad looks well but has put on a few pounds
The pond	thinks it is cool pond with lots of frogs, thinks that Granddad must love his pond because there are three paintings of it in the house	thinks it is a beautiful pond and mentions the heavy rain that brought all the frogs out
Plans for the next day	train to London with Granddad, Wax Museum, the War Museum, and maybe the Science Museum, the London Eye	sorting Mum's things

2. Answers will vary.

EXTENSIONS

- Other texts involving letters include the following:
  - *Letters from the Inside* by John Marsden
  - *Annushka's Voyage* by Edith Tarbescu (picture book)
  - *Flour Babies* by Anne Fine

TWO LETTERS

Name _____

Read the two letters, written to the same person and answer the questions on the following pages.

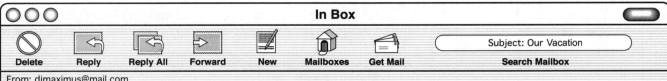

In Box

Delete   Reply   Reply All   Forward   New   Mailboxes   Get Mail   Subject: Our Vacation   Search Mailbox

From: djmaximus@mail.com

To: Mike.Corby@mail.com
From: djmaximus@mail.com
Subject: Our Vacation

Hi, Dad!

I'm in an Internet cafe in Croydon! It has a coffee shop in it—that's where Mom is (of course!). We caught the train from right outside Granddad's place.

It was pretty uncomfortable on the plane. Luckily they had computer games and music channels with headphones—otherwise I might have gone a bit crazy from boredom. You were right about the plane food—yuck! They gave me the kids' meals, which was a bit embarrassing. Mine came with mini-chocolate bars though.

Granddad's house is a two-story and very skinny. It's in the middle of two other houses, and they all look exactly the same. (I'm glad our houses aren't joined together like that, otherwise we'd get lots of complaints from the neighbors about my music!)

Granddad likes wearing ties and he smells like soap. He has LOTS of stamps!! He goes to stamp auctions and buys big bags of them and sorts them. He finds rare ones by using an ultraviolet light to look for invisible marks. He looks like a forensic scientist searching for fingerprints.

Out the back is a cool pond with loads of frogs! There were heaps of tadpoles in the water, too, and piles of little eggs. Granddad must love his pond! He has three paintings of it in the house—I think Nan painted them.

Tomorrow, Granddad and I are catching the train to London! We are going to go to the Wax Museum, the War Museum, and maybe the Science Museum, too (hopefully we won't have time for that last one). We are also going on the London Eye, which is this huge Ferris wheel that looks out over London. I can't wait!

Don't forget to take Mitch for a walk EVERY day, please. Have fun without us!

Max

March 25

Dear Mike,

How are you? I hope you are not working too hard while we are away. I expect the healthy dinners in the freezer to be eaten by the time we return (and not too many pizza boxes in the trash!).

The flight was long and Max played computer games and wore headphones for most of the trip—leaving me with no one to talk to! We dragged our luggage onto the busy public transport system and finally arrived at Dad's. I could see immediately that things had changed. The hedges are overgrown and the front garden is in dire need of weeding. Dad looks well, but I think he has put on a few pounds. Too many of those cream cakes that Mum used to ban him from. I've warned him about the history of diabetes in our family.

Dad showed Max his stamp collection and his pond. A heavy rain last night brought all the frogs out! It really is a beautiful pond. Dad is managing to take care of that part of the garden well. I crept upstairs while they were outside and saw Mum's clothes still hanging in the closet. It took my breath away to see her things sitting just as she had left them on her dresser, too. Poor Dad. Tomorrow, while he takes Max to London for the day, I'll start sorting Mum's things out. I really miss her, Mike, and I wish Max could have met her.

I look forward to seeing you in three weeks. I wish you were here.

Love, Kathy

TWO LETTERS

Literal — Find the answers directly in the text.

Read each sentence. Answer **Yes** or **No**.

1. Max enjoys listening to music. ☐ Yes ☐ No

2. Ultraviolet light shows marks on stamps invisible to the human eye. ☐ Yes ☐ No

3. Max had met his grandfather previously. ☐ Yes ☐ No

4. The rain brought the frogs out. ☐ Yes ☐ No

5. Max is looking forward to going to the science museum. ☐ Yes ☐ No

6. Kathy's mother was a painter. ☐ Yes ☐ No

Inferential — Think about what the text says.

1. Why do you think Kathy's breath was "taken away" when she went upstairs?

_____

_____

_____

2. Why do you think Granddad has been taking such good care of the pond?

_____

_____

_____

3. Do you think this trip is more than a vacation? What might be its other purpose?

_____

_____

_____

TWO LETTERS

Applied   Use what you know about the text and your own experience.

1. How old do you think Max is?

_____

2. What type of person is Kathy?

_____

_____

_____

_____

_____

_____

3. How do you think Granddad is feeling about this visit from his family?

_____

_____

_____

_____

_____

_____

4. Why do you think Mike didn't go with them on this trip?

_____

_____

_____

TWO LETTERS

Use the text on page 60 to complete the following activities.

1. The characters Kathy and Max, are on the same trip but have different experiences. Make comparisons between the two characters' experiences by writing about each of these events.

Event	Max	Kathy
Seeing Granddad's house		
Seeing Granddad		
The pond		
Plans for the next day		

2. When you read a story, your memories of your experiences, people who you know, and the things you have read about or seen in movies can be "triggered." This is called "making connections" with the text. What connections did you make when you read "Two Letters"? Complete the sentences below.

Making Connections

a. *The story reminds me of a time when* _____

_____

_____ .

b. *The character reminds me of* _____

because _____

_____ .

c. *I think knowing something about* _____

helped me to understand the text because _____

_____

_____

_____ .

Genre: Fairy Tale

READING FOCUS

- Analyzes and extracts information from a fairy tale to answer literal, inferential, and applied questions
- Makes comparisons between a character in a text and himself/herself
- Makes comparisons between a well-known fairy tale and the one given
- Makes connections between the information in the text and his/her own world

ANSWER KEY

Literal (Page 66)

1. He defeated Warren the Small, rescued the city of Marc, and also had the highest score.

2. Hex must rescue the isolated city of Hur from the clutches of Nigel the Giant.

3. "Once upon a time" and "lived happily ever after"

Inferential (Page 66)

1. The three wishes Hex made were a custom-built computer, Sapira the Gorgeous at his side, and a sportscar.

2. Torrin was already in the caverns because he was the spy that had slipped in.

3. You can tell Hex liked and used his technological gadgets because he was good at playing video games and he used his mobile phone to help him with his assignment.

4. The characters are given such names to show/describe their attributes.

Applied (Page 67)

1–2. Answers will vary.

Applying Strategies (Page 68)

1–3. Answers will vary.

EXTENSIONS

- Students may wish to research and read fairy tales from other countries.
- Students may like to read titles such as the following:
  - *Once Upon a More Enlightened Time* by James Finn Garner
  - *The Enchanted Forest Chronicles* by Patricia C. Wrede
  - *Book of Enchantments* by Patricia C. Wrede
- Read *Roald Dahl's Revolting Rhymes* by Roald Dahl to the students, and encourage them to write their own fractured fairy tales.

HEX AND THE CAPTIVE CITY OF HUR

Name _____

Read the fairy tale and answer the questions on the following pages.

Once upon a time, in the land of Tech, a cute computer technician named Hex sat quietly, gaming on his trusted machine.

With his usual finesse and poise, he quickly defeated the villain Warren the Small and rescued the doomed city of Marc and its beautiful queen, Sapira the Gorgeous.

As he began to exit the game, a flash of spiraling lights filled the screen, immediately replaced by the flawless face of Sapira the Gorgeous.

Hex stared in shock as she began to speak.

"Because of your heroic deeds (and a score better than anybody else!), you have been chosen to receive three wishes. You may have anything your heart desires, but first you must complete an assignment."

"Your assignment, should you accept it, is to rescue the isolated city of Hur from the clutches of Nigel the Giant. We managed to slip a spy, Torrin the Quick, into the city before contact was lost. Nigel the Giant has thrown the elite guards into the dungeon caverns and placed a beast at the entrance to guard them. Defer is a monstrous dog with an enormous appetite, and he never sleeps. If you could contact Torrin the Quick and enlist his help, the elite guards will be able to overtake Nigel's small group of trained warriors, and the city will be freed."

"Sure, Sapira! I can't foresee any problem. I'll give it a try! I have my three wishes all figured out! You can consider the deed done!" replied Hex.

Quickly, he grabbed his mobile phone and scrolled through the numbers he had stored. He selected the ones he wanted and dialed. Instantly, he found himself inside the caverns, standing next to Torrin the Quick.

"Hey, muscles! I'm Hex and we're about to depart this place!" he confidently stated.

He dialed again, and as if by magic, a pizza delivery person appeared just outside the entrance.

"One barbecue meatlovers for someone named Hex!" he bellowed.

"Over here," replied Hex, "right in front of this enormous beast!"

Defer, who had never experienced the delight of a barbecue meatlovers pizza before, gobbled it up as though it was his last meal!

Soothing music from Hex's smartphone drifted around the caverns, and Defer was lulled into blissful sleep with his stomach full of pizza.

"Well, Torrin. I've done my part. The rest is up to you," Hex said as he reached for his mobile phone once more, dialed, and disappeared from sight.

Torrin the Quick released the elite guards, who overthrew the warriors of Nigel the Giant and freed the city of Hur.

Hex lived happily ever after, busily gaming on his custom-built computer with Sapira the Gorgeous at his side and his sportscar decorating the driveway.

It just goes to show what technology and a good tip for the pizza-delivery person can achieve!

HEX AND THE CAPTIVE CITY OF HUR

Literal   Find the answers directly in the text.

1. Why was Hex chosen for the assignment by Queen Sapira?

   _____

   _____

2. What assignment must Hex complete to get his three wishes?

   _____

   _____

3. Which words in the text tell you that this is a fairy tale?

   _____

   _____

Inferential   Think about what the text says.

1. What were the three wishes that Hex made? _____

   _____

2. Why was Torrin already in the caverns? _____

   _____

3. How do you know that Hex liked and used his technological gadgets? _____

   _____

4. Why are the characters given such names as Nigel the Giant, Torrin the Quick, Sapira the Gorgeous, and Warren the Small?

   _____

   _____

HEX AND THE CAPTIVE CITY OF HUR

Applied   Use what you know about the text and your own experience.

1. Why do you think the author uses technology as the basis for this modern fairy tale?

_____

_____

_____

_____

_____

_____

_____

_____

2. What would your three wishes be?

_____

_____

_____

_____

_____

_____

_____

_____

_____

_____

Name _____

HEX AND THE CAPTIVE CITY OF HUR

Comparing

This page should be used in conjunction with the fairy tale on page 65.

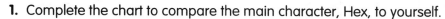

1. Complete the chart to compare the main character, Hex, to yourself.

Similarities	Differences

2. Select a familiar fairy tale and compare it to the one on page 65 using the categories given.

Familiar Fairy Tale	Hex and the Captive City of Hur
Setting	
Characters	
Plot	
Ending	
Language Used	

3. Write sentences to compare your leisure activities with those of the main character, Hex. If your pursuits are very similar to Hex's, is this a good or bad thing? Why?

Making Connections

_____

_____

_____

_____

Genre: Play

READING FOCUS

- Analyzes and extracts information from a play to answer literal, inferential, and applied questions
- Uses sensory imaging to describe a setting from a character's point of view

---

ANSWER KEY

Literal (Page 71)

1. She has reached the end of the tunnel.
2. The trapdoor has suddenly flown open.
3. He hears a scream.
4. He thinks they have traveled back in time.

Inferential (Page 71)

1. a. Answers will vary. Possible answer(s): surprised, relieved, hopeful, uncertain.
   b. Answers will vary. Possible answer(s): weary, uncertain, scared, curious.
   c. Answers will vary. Possible answer(s): scared, panicked, frightened.
2. The noise is coming from the angry-looking people who are chasing Jake and Sasha.
3. the feeling of eagerness, fright, thrill, excitement, apprehension

Applied (Page 72)

Answers will vary.

Applying Strategies (Page 73)

1–2. Answers will vary.

EXTENSIONS

- Look for plays adapted from popular children's books. Some suggested titles include the following:
  - *Charlie and the Chocolate Factory* by Roald Dahl
  - *Hating Alison Ashley* by Robin Klein
  - *The Lion, the Witch and the Wardrobe* by C.S. Lewis

THE SECRET BOOK

Name _____

Read the play and answer the questions on the following pages.

Sasha and Jake are sister and brother. One day, they open an old book at their grandmother's house and are suddenly transported to a dirt road, where they are chased by a bunch of angry-looking people. Sasha and Jake make their way into a tunnel into the side of a hill and run in the dim light . . .

Jake *(panting)* Sasha! I can hear them. They must be right at the entrance . . .

Sasha comes to an abrupt halt. Jake crashes into her.

Jake Hey! Don't stop! They'll find the tunnel any second now.

Sasha feels in her pocket for a flashlight and switches it on. The illumination reveals the end of the tunnel.

Sasha *(quietly)* We're trapped, Jake.

Shouting and yelling is heard from farther up the tunnel. Jake and Sasha look at each other with fear in their eyes.

Sasha They can't be far behind us now. Who are they?

Jake There were pictures of people just like them in that book of Grandma's, remember? It was about people who lived hundreds of years ago.

Sasha That's impossible, Jake. That would mean we've . . .

Jake . . . traveled back in time.

They fall silent. The noises are growing louder. Jake frantically scrabbles at the walls.

Jake A tunnel that goes nowhere doesn't make any sense!

Sasha stares at him.

Sasha You're right, Jake! There has to be a way out of here!

Jake But the walls are solid. *(He feels above his head.)* And so is the ceiling. *(He whimpers.)* They're going to catch us.

Sasha Wait. There's one place we haven't tried. *(She shines the light on the floor of the tunnel and kicks at the ground.)* There's something here.

Sasha drops to her knees and quickly unearths a metal ring.

Jake It's a trapdoor!

Sasha throws down the flashlight. They both pull on the ring. The trapdoor flies open, sending them tumbling backwards. Sasha fumbles for the flashlight and peers into the hole.

Sasha There's a rope.

Jake *(peering over her shoulder)* What do you think is down there?

The noises are now very loud.

Sasha I don't know, but it's got to be better than dealing with those angry people. *(She hands the flashlight to Jake.)* I'll go first.

Sasha takes a deep breath and lowers herself down the rope. Jake hears a scream. He falls to his knees, peering into the hole.

Jake Sasha!

THE SECRET BOOK

Find the answers directly in the text.

1. Why does Sasha come to an abrupt halt? _____

_____

2. Why do Jake and Sasha tumble backwards? _____

_____

3. Why does Jake fall to his knees and peer into the hole? _____

_____

4. What does Jake think has happened to him and Sasha? _____

_____

Inferential   Think about what the text says.

1. List words that describe how Jake might feel as he says each of these lines.

    a. "It's a trapdoor!" _____

    b. "What do you think is down there?" _____

    c. "They're going to catch us." _____

2. Who or what is making the noise coming from farther down the tunnel?

_____

_____

3. The noises coming from farther down the tunnel are mentioned three times in the play, each time getting louder. Explain what effect this is designed to produce.

_____

_____

_____

THE SECRET BOOK

Applied   Use what you know about the text and your own experience.

Why do you think Sasha screams? Write three scenarios. Include some dialogue between the two characters.

- _____
  _____
  _____
  _____
  _____
  _____

- _____
  _____
  _____
  _____
  _____

- _____
  _____
  _____
  _____
  _____

Name _____

THE SECRET BOOK

You are a children's author. You are asked to turn the play excerpt you have just read into a narrative. The first thing you need to do is make the setting more vivid for your readers. You can do this by thinking about what a character might be experiencing through his/her senses.

1. **a.** Choose one of the characters from the play. ☐ Jake ☐ Sasha

    b. Focus on the moment that the flashlight reveals the end of the tunnel. Now, write notes under each heading below. You can use the hints to help you think of more ideas.

What can your character see? Hints: Is the tunnel rocky? Is the light strong or weak? Is the other character's face visible?	**What can your character hear?** Hints: Is there water dripping? Can he/she hear his/her own breathing?
What can your character smell? Hints: Is the air musty? Are there any animals living in the tunnel?	**What can your character touch/feel?** Hints: Is the tunnel cold? Is the ground uneven?

2. Use your ideas to describe the setting from your character's point of view.

_____
_____
_____
_____
_____
_____
_____
_____

Genre: Fable

READING FOCUS

- Analyzes and extracts information from fables to answer literal, inferential, and applied questions
- Determines the important features of fables and uses these to write his/her own modern fable

ANSWER KEY

Literal (Page 76)

1. Answers will vary. Possible answer(s):
   a. bucket   b. bottle, container   c. stick, pole   d. murmured, mumbled
2. a. buy some sheep.
   b. The milkmaid tossed her head and . . . /The pail fell and . . .
   c. the fox woke up and raced off.
   d. The poor man raised his staff above his head and . . .

Inferential (Page 76)

1. A moral is a type of lesson about life.
2. Answers should indicate to not depend on something until you actually possess it.
3. Answers will vary. Possible answer(s): All the characters got ahead of themselves and all assumed that good things were coming their way, when none of it was certain to happen.

Applied (Page 77)

Answers/drawings will vary.

Applying Strategies (Page 78)

1.

Title	The Milkmaid and Her Pail	The Boy and the Fox	The Poor Man and the Flask of Oil
Setting	milkmaid walking to the dairy	forest	poor man staring at a flask on the shelf
Main Character	milkmaid	boy	poor man
Number of Characters	1	2	1
Important Object(s)	pail of milk	rye and fox	flask of oil, staff
Plot	☑ Simple ☐ Complex	☑ Simple ☐ Complex	☑ Simple ☐ Complex
Plot Summary	Milkmaid was daydreaming about all the possibilities and forgot the milk on her head. She tossed her head back, and the pail fell to the ground, spilling the milk.	A village boy spotted a sleeping fox and planned to capture the fox and sell the skin. The boy got carried away with his ideas, screamed, and woke the fox up, who ran off into the forest.	A poor man was admiring a flask of oil sitting on the shelf that a kind merchant gave him. He got carried away talking about all the good things that he thought were coming his way. He raised the staff and knocked the flask of oil to the ground.
Moral (in your own words)	Answers will vary.	Answers will vary.	Answers will vary.

2–3. Answers will vary.

EXTENSIONS

- Some of Aesop's fables that students may enjoy reading include the following:
  - "Androcles and the Lion"
  - "The Monkey and the Dolphin"
  - "The Mouse, the Frog, and the Hawk"
- Other well-known authors of fables include Phaedrus, Babrius, and Bidpai.

DON'T COUNT YOUR CHICKENS!

Name _____

Read the fables and answer the questions on the following pages.

The Milkmaid and Her Pail (from Ancient Greece – Aesop)

Once there was a milkmaid who daydreamed as she walked to the dairy, carrying a pail of milk on her head.

"The milk in my pail will give me cream, which I'll make into butter and sell at the market," she thought to herself. "I'll buy some eggs with the money, and those will give me chicks. When the chicks have grown, I'll sell some of them. With the money I make, I'll buy myself a beautiful dress. I'll wear the dress to the fair, and all the young men will admire me. But I won't take any notice of them. I'll toss my head and keep walking."

The milkmaid forgot about the pail of milk and tossed her head. The pail fell to the ground, spilling all the milk.

Moral: Don't count your chickens before they hatch.

The Boy and the Fox (from Sweden)

There once was a village boy who was walking through the forest near his home. He saw a fox lying in a clearing, fast asleep.

"I could capture that fox and sell the skin," the boy muttered to himself. "With the money I get for it, I'll buy some rye and sow it in my father's field. All the people in the village will see it when they pass by and they'll say, 'Look at that wonderful rye!' I'll say to them, 'Get away from my rye!' But they won't listen. So I'll have to yell, 'Get away from my rye!' But they'll still ignore me. So I'll have to run up to them and say it even louder."

The boy became so involved in his ideas that he took a deep breath and screamed, "GET AWAY FROM MY RYE!"

The noise woke up the fox, who raced off into the forest before the boy even had time to move.

Moral: It's best to take what you can reach, for of undone deeds you should never screech.

The Poor Man and the Flask of Oil (from India)

Once, a poor man was given a flask of oil by a kind merchant. The poor man put the flask on a shelf and stared at it.

"If I sold that oil, maybe there would be enough to buy some sheep. The sheep would have lambs, and soon I would have a large flock. If I sold some of the sheep, I would be rich enough to marry. My wife would have a son, and he'd grow to be strong and handsome. But if he was disobedient, I would have to raise my staff to him."

The man got so carried away that he raised his staff above his head. The staff knocked the flask of oil to the ground, where it broke. The oil was lost.

DON'T COUNT YOUR CHICKENS!

Literal   Find the answers directly in the text.

1. Write another word with a similar meaning for each of these words from the text.

   a. pail _____   **b.** flask _____

   c. staff _____   **d.** muttered _____

2. Complete the "cause and effect" table.

Cause	Effect
a. The poor man thought he would sell the oil and . . .	
b.	the milk spilled on the ground.
c. The boy screamed out and . . .	
d.	the flask was knocked off the shelf.

Inferential   Think about what the text says.

1. A fable is a story that tells a moral. What do you think a moral is?

_____

_____

2. Write a suitable moral for "The Poor Man and the Flask of Oil."

_____

_____

3. What do the main characters of these fables have in common?

_____

_____

DON'T COUNT YOUR CHICKENS!

Choose one of the fables and turn it into a cartoon of five or fewer frames. Think carefully about what should go into each frame before you begin.

Title: _____

1.

2.

3.

4.

5.

DON'T COUNT YOUR CHICKENS!

Determining Importance

The three fables on page 75 come from three different countries, yet they are similar in many ways.

1. Complete the table for each of the fables.

Title	The Milkmaid and her Pail	The Boy and the Fox	The Poor Man and the Flask of Oil
Setting			
Main Character			
Number of Characters			
Important Object(s)			
Plot	☐ Simple ☐ Complex	☐ Simple ☐ Complex	☐ Simple ☐ Complex
Plot Summary			
Moral (in your own words)			

2. List the features you discovered the fables had in common.

_____

_____

_____

_____

_____

3. On a separate sheet of paper, use these common features to help you write a modern version of one of the three fables. Include a modern version of its moral!

Genre: Report

READING FOCUS

- Analyzes and extracts information from a report to answer literal, inferential, and applied questions
- Scans text to locate keywords and phrases to summarize information
- Determines the importance of information within a text by writing a main idea statement

ANSWER KEY

Literal (Page 81)

1. c   2. b   3. c

Inferential (Page 81)

1. According to legend, St. Patrick, along with God's help, drove all the venomous snakes in Ireland into the sea, where they drowned.

2. The Irish word for hillocks and mounds is *sidhe*, where fairies are said to inhabit. **Sidhe**og contains *sidhe* in the first part of the word.

3. Answers will vary. Possible answer(s): to get the "Irish gift of the Blarney"

4. Answers will vary. Possbile answer(s): it's the most famous symbol in Ireland, the legend is popular in Ireland, a majority of the population in Ireland are Catholics.

Applied (Page 82)

1–3. Answers will vary.

Applying Strategies (Page 83)

Legend	Keywords and Phrases	Main Idea
Irish Fairy Folk	*sidheog*, *sidhe*, Tuatha de Dannan, magical powers, Tuatha defeated by the Milesians, lived underground	It is believed that the *sidheog* live in *sidhe* and disturbing them will bring bad luck.
The Leprechaun	tiny old man, green tunic with a green hat, hidden pot of gold	Legend has it that if you catch a leprechaun, he'll lead you to his pot of gold—if you don't take your eyes off him.
The Banshee	long, flowing silver-gray hair; long gray-white cloak; pale skin; red eyes; cries outside of the houses; perish	The Banshee cries outside the houses of people who are about to perish.
St. Patrick	patron saint, venomous snakes, drowned	Legend has it that St. Patrick drove all the venomous snakes into the sea, where they drowned.
The Blarney Stone	Blarney Castle, kissing the stone, "Irish gift of the Blarney"	Legend has it that people who kiss the stone will be given the "Irish gift of the Blarney."
The Shamrock	three-leaved, Holy Trinity, national flower	St. Patrick used the shamrock to help explain the Holy Trinity to his followers.

EXTENSIONS

- Students can report on two other Irish legends—the "Wearing of the Green" and the Claddagh Ring.
- If students are interested in Irish legends and mythology, the much-loved Irish fairy tale "The Children of Lir" can be found on page 35.

IRISH LEGENDS

Name _____

Read the report about Irish legends and answer the questions on the following pages.

A legend is a story with its origin based on an actual event in the past.

Irish Fairy Folk

The Irish word for fairy is *sidheog* (pronounced *sheehog*). Fairies are believed to live in hillocks or mounds (*sidhe*), and it is said that touching or disturbing them will bring bad luck. Their origin goes back to the time Ireland was ruled by the highly regarded Tuatha de Dannan—an intelligent race of people who many considered to have magical powers or even to be gods. However, after battles against invading forces over a period of 200 years, the Tuatha were eventually defeated by the Milesians. The Milesians allowed the Tuatha to remain in Ireland but only if they lived underground . . . and so began the legend of the fairy folk.

The Leprechaun

The most well-known Irish fairy is the leprechaun. According to legend, he looks like a tiny old man, wears a green tunic and a green hat, can be found sitting under a tree mending fairies' shoes, and possesses a hidden pot of gold. It is said that if you catch a leprechaun, he will lead you to his pot of gold—but only if you don't take your eyes off him! Otherwise, he will vanish into thin air.

The Banshee

A banshee is a type of female fairy woman. She has long, flowing silver-gray hair and wears a long, gray-white cloak over her thin body. Her skin is pale, and her eyes are red from crying. This is because it is believed she cries and wails outside the houses of people who are about to perish. The wailing sound is a dreaded warning.

St. Patrick

St. Patrick is the patron saint of Ireland. Around 430 CE, Patrick went to Ireland to spread Catholicism. (Today, a majority of Ireland's population are Catholic.)

Several legends are associated with St. Patrick. Probably the most well-known being the story that, with God's help, he drove all the venomous snakes in Ireland into the sea, where they drowned. To this day, there are no venomous snakes in Ireland.

The Blarney Stone

The Blarney Stone is set in a wall of Blarney Castle, located in the Irish village of the same name. Kissing the stone is said to give the kisser the "Irish gift of the Blarney," which is the ability to speak eloquently and persuasively but in such a manner that it is not offensive. One legend claims that the stone's powers came from an old woman who rewarded a king of the castle after he saved her from drowning.

To kiss the stone, you have to lie on your back and bend backwards and downwards, holding on to iron bars for support!

The Irish Shamrock

The name *shamrock* comes from an Irish word meaning "three-leaved." According to legend, St. Patrick used the common clover plant to help explain the meaning of the Holy Trinity (Father, Son, and Holy Spirit as one being) to his followers. The shamrock is the national flower of Ireland and its most famous symbol.

IRISH LEGENDS

Literal   Find the answers directly in the text.

1. The legend of the Irish fairy folk began with . . .

   a. ☐ the Irish.

   b. ☐ the Milesians.

   c. ☐ the Tuatha de Dannan.

2. A leprechaun looks like . . .

   a. ☐ a small man.

   b. ☐ a tiny old man.

   c. ☐ a small young man.

3. A banshee has . . .

   a. ☐ silver-gray hair, dark skin, red eyes.

   b. ☐ silver-gray hair, pale skin, blue eyes.

   c. ☐ silver-gray hair, red eyes, pale skin.

Inferential   Think about what the text says.

1. According to legend, why are there no venomous snakes in Ireland?

   _____

   _____

2. Why do you think the Irish word for fairy is *sidheog*?

   _____

   _____

3. Thousands of tourists a year visit Blarney Castle to kiss the stone. Why do you think this is?

   _____

   _____

4. Why do you think the shamrock was chosen as Ireland's national flower?

   _____

   _____

IRISH LEGENDS

| **Applied** | Use what you know about the text and your own experience. |

1. There have been no reports of finding a leprechaun's pot of gold.
   Why do you think this is so?

   _____

   _____

   _____

   _____

   _____

   _____

2. How do you think the legend of the banshee might have begun?

   _____

   _____

   _____

   _____

   _____

   _____

   _____

3. If you traveled to Ireland, would you visit Blarney Castle and kiss the Blarney Stone?
   Explain your answer.

   _____

   _____

   _____

   _____

   _____

   _____

IRISH LEGENDS

Use the text on page 80 to complete the activity. Scan the text to find keywords and phrases. Write these next to each legend to summarize the information. Use the information you recorded to describe the main idea for each legend.

Legend	Keywords and Phrases	Main Idea
Irish Fairy Folk		
The Leprechaun		
The Banshee		
St. Patrick		
The Blarney Stone		
The Shamrock		

Genre: Biography

READING FOCUS

- Analyzes and extracts information from a biography to answer literal, inferential, and applied questions
- Discriminates between important and less important information contained in a text
- Identifies key information contained in a text to write a summary

ANSWER KEY

Literal (Page 86)

1. Fact   2. Fact   3. Opinion   4. Fact   5. Opinion

Inferential (Page 86)

1. Chronic fatigue syndrome affects people's physical and mental energy.

2. Layne promotes women's surfing and encourages girls, and all athletes, to pursue their dreams.

3. Answers will vary. Possible answer(s): determination, hard worker, disciplined.

4. Layne worked hard to pursue her dream in a male-dominated sport.

5. Answers will vary. Possible answer(s): Layne had to work even harder physically and mentally. She had to listen to her body.

Applied (Page 87)

1–2. Answers will vary.

Applying Strategies (Page 88)

1–3. Answers will vary.

EXTENSIONS

- Using the Internet, look up the biographies for the following elite surfers:
  - Kelly Slater
  - Mark Occhilupo
  - Taj Burrows
  - Carissa Moore
  - Bethany Hamilton
  - Laird Hamilton
  - Stephanie Gilmore
  - Lakey Peterson

Name _____

Read the biography and answer the questions on the following pages.

Name: Layne Beachley

Nickname: "Gidget" or "Beach"

Born: Sydney, Australia on May 24, 1972

Lives: Northshore, Hawaii/Sydney, Australia

Turned professional: 16 years old

Accomplishments: Seven-time ASP World Champion

Trademark moves: Big-wave riding

Layne was adopted by Neil and Valerie Beachley at six weeks old. When Layne was four, Layne's dad gave her a surfboard. She had already been skateboarding for a year prior to this and soon discovered she was good at surfing, too.

Growing up in Sydney, Australia, Layne played soccer and tennis and would ride her bicycle to Manly Beach to teach herself to surf. While in high school, Layne entered and won the regional scholastic surfing title. She placed among the state of New South Wales' best high-school surfers. She went on to win competitions and placed fifth in the nationals. By the time Layne was 16, her talent and determination found her competing in professional surfing competitions around Australia.

Layne completed her high school degree and for the next four years worked up to four part-time jobs a week to save the money needed to finance her surfing ambition and to be able to compete overseas.

By 20, Layne was ranked number 6 in the world. She started vigorous fitness and strength training that would give her the edge over other women surfers. She continued winning competitions and discovered success in the "big wave" events. Layne would challenge 30-foot waves—the height of a three-story building—and conquer them! Layne celebrated her 21st birthday and claimed her first World Tour victory.

In 1993 and 1996, Layne was afflicted by chronic fatigue syndrome. She worked hard, listening to her body, trying to determine what gave her the physical and mental energy to get out of bed each day. Although Layne considered giving up surfing, she persevered and overcame the disease each time.

By 1998 Layne had won five out of the 11 World Championship events. She was a major competitor, earning the most prize money by a woman surfer in a single season in 1998.

Layne continued to dominate the women's surfing circuit. She won six consecutive World Championships from 1998 to 2003, and again in 2006—a feat never achieved before by any surfer, male or female.

One of Layne's goals has always been to promote women's surfing and to encourage girls to pursue their dreams, whether they have sporting, cultural, or academic goals. In 1993, Layne created the Aim for the Stars Foundation, which offers financial grants and support to girls with big dreams.

Layne also runs surfing clinics and speaks publicly to young people. In 2003, Layne joined UNICEF, helping the organization raise awareness of the need for safe drinking water around the globe. In 2004, Layne Beachley was awarded the Australian Female Athlete of the Year.

In March, 2005, at age 32, Layne was the runner-up at the Margaret River Masters, in Perth, Western Australia. Layne retired from full-time competition in 2010.

A SURFING CHAMPION

Literal Find the answers directly in the text.

Read each sentence. Decide if each statement is a **Fact** or **Opinion**.

1. Layne began skateboarding at the age of three. ☐ Fact ☐ Opinion

2. By 16, Layne was surfing in national competitions. ☐ Fact ☐ Opinion

3. Layne prefers the big-wave events because there is less competition. ☐ Fact ☐ Opinion

4. In 1998, Layne earned more prize money than any other female surfer in one season. ☐ Fact ☐ Opinion

5. Young people can achieve anything if they work hard enough. ☐ Fact ☐ Opinion

Inferential Think about what the text says.

1. How are people with chronic fatigue syndrome affected?

   _____

2. How does Layne Beachley use her profile and success to benefit others?

   _____

3. Which personal traits does Layne possess, enabling her to achieve such great success in her life?

   _____

4. What factors in Layne's own life do you think inspired her to create the Aim for the Stars Foundation?

   _____

5. How do you think Layne's chronic fatigue syndrome affected her career?

   _____

   _____

   _____

A SURFING CHAMPION

Applied   Use what you know about the text and your own experience.

1. Layne Beachley is considered to be a role model for young people. Do you agree? Explain your answer.

_____

_____

_____

_____

_____

_____

_____

_____

_____

2. Write about another role model and his/her accomplishments. How has this role model inspired you?

_____

_____

_____

_____

_____

_____

_____

_____

_____

A SURFING CHAMPION

 **Summarizing**

Identifying keywords and phrases in a text and then summarizing that information are important skills to learn—and they take practice! You are going to condense the biography about Layne Beachley into one paragraph of information.

1. Reread the text. Underline keywords and phrases.

2. Sort the words and phrases you have underlined by placing them in one of the following categories. Use bullet-point form to record the information.

The Main Idea(s)	Other Important Facts	Incidental (Less Important) Facts

3. Use the information above to write one paragraph that summarizes the life of Layne Beachley.

_____

_____

_____

_____

_____

_____

_____

Genre: Journalistic Writing— Newspaper Report

READING FOCUS

- Analyzes and extracts information from a journalistic report to answer literal, inferential, and applied questions
- Scans text to locate words and to find contextual information to assist in determining meaning
- Paraphrases understanding of a word meaning before writing it and consulting a dictionary

ANSWER KEY

Literal (Page 91)

1. False	2. False	3. True	4. True
5. False	6. False	7. True	

Inferential (Page 91)

1. members of the press and the general public who were trespassing to see the site for themselves

2. Answers will vary. Possible answer(s): Yes, the local people were happy because business was booming; no, the local people were not happy because the commotion disrupted their way of life.

3. Answers will vary. Possible answer(s): Yes, the police were justified because the land is private property, and people trespassing should be prosecuted.

Applied (Page 92)

1–4. Answers will vary.

Applying Strategies (Page 93)

1–5. Answers will vary.

EXTENSIONS

- Collect newspaper reports and sort them into categories (e.g., sports, business, human-interest stories, crime, and social events). Discuss similarities and differences.
- Discuss the importance of headlines and headers—what they aim to do and what makes them successful or unsuccessful.

Name _____

Read the journalistic report and answer the questions on the following pages.

BARE TREES BAFFLE LOCAL FARMER

A most unusual, and it would appear inexplicable, phenomenon causes concern to the small community of Cosgrove.

Last Friday, local farmer James Wilson observed that a clump of approximately 12 trees growing in the southeast corner of his property were stripped of foliage and covered with a strange, white, sticky substance. The concerned farmer was even more baffled to discover a circle of brown, burnt earth nearby—and that there wasn't a leaf to be seen on the ground.

Fearing some exotic disease and the possibility of it spreading and infecting other plants, he contacted the Forestry Department, who visited the site and declared that the trees were healthy and disease-free. On their advice, he then contacted the Agriculture Department to ensure that the problem wasn't the result of an insect plague. They were unable to find anything to suggest that insects were the cause.

Local interest is growing, and wild and varied theories and explanations are being discussed. Locals are visiting the site in droves, looking for evidence of alien spaceships, human intervention, or some natural phenomenon. There seems to be little evidence to support any of their theories to date.

As the mystery deepens, visitors from farther afield are also descending on this previously quiet rural retreat. Local businesses are booming as they struggle to provide sufficient accommodations, food, and services for the hordes of urban invaders.

James Wilson is not enjoying his notoriety. He is refusing to answer his telephone. The gate at the end of the dirt road leading to his farmhouse has a huge padlock on it and prominently displays a large sign with the very clear message that visitors are unwelcome. Undeterred, curious members of the press and the general public are ignoring his attempts to discourage their unwanted attention and are swarming across all barriers to inspect the site for themselves. Mr. Wilson now has to contend with rounding up stray stock that has wandered off because gates have been left open; extinguishing small fires lit by campers; repairing fences; and collecting a multitude of bottles, cans, and other trash discarded by inconsiderate, unwelcome visitors.

Last night, Mr. Wilson appeared on a local television program and said that "there was nothing to see" and that he just wanted his quiet life back. He added that he regretted that he had ever "opened his big mouth," that it was all "a big fuss about nothing," and that he wished it would all "just go away."

Local police have appealed to the public to come forward with any reliable information that could help to explain the mystery or lead to the apprehension of any person or persons responsible. Otherwise, they should respect Mr. Wilson's request for privacy and refrain from trespassing on his property. Police further warned that any future trespassers would be prosecuted. They intend to erect signs to this effect and to provide regular patrols to ensure compliance.

Farmer James Wilson surveys his mystery trees.

BARE TREES BAFFLE LOCAL FARMER

Literal   Find the answers directly in the text.

Read each sentence. Decide if each statement is **True** or **False**.

1. There was a circle of white earth around the trees.   ☐ True ☐ False

2. James Wilson enjoyed the publicity.   ☐ True ☐ False

3. The Forestry Department recommended that the   ☐ True ☐ False
    farmer should contact the Agriculture Department.

4. The visitors ignored Mr. Wilson's sign.   ☐ True ☐ False

5. The visitors took care of Mr. Wilson's property.   ☐ True ☐ False

6. Mr. Wilson appeared on television because he wanted   ☐ True ☐ False
    to publicize what had happened on his farm.

7. The police believe that it is possible that someone may   ☐ True ☐ False
    have caused the damage to the trees.

Inferential   Think about what the text says.

1. Who do you think broke Farmer Wilson's fences?

    _____

    _____

2. Do you think that the local people were happy about the publicity their town was attracting?
    Explain why you think this.

    _____

    _____

    _____

3. Were the police justified in taking the action they did? Why or why not?

    _____

    _____

    _____

BARE TREES BAFFLE LOCAL FARMER

Applied   Use what you know about the text and your own experience.

1. Do you think people will take any notice of the signs the police are going to erect? Give reasons for your answer.

   _____

   _____

   _____

   _____

2. What do you think will happen next at Cosgrove?

   _____

   _____

   _____

   _____

3. What do you think could have caused the mysterious phenomenon?

   _____

   _____

   _____

   _____

4. If you were James Wilson, how would you feel about all the attention?

   _____

   _____

   _____

   _____

   _____

Name _____

Applying Strategies

BARE TREES BAFFLE LOCAL FARMER

Scanning

Complete the chart of interesting words from the text on page 90.

1. Select and write six words that you find interesting from the text.

2. Identify the paragraph in which the word is used.

3. Read the sentence to help with finding a possible meaning.

4. Write *your* definition of the word.

5. Consult a dictionary, then write the definition provided in the dictionary.

Word	Paragraph	My Definition	Dictionary Definition

©*Teacher Created Resources* 93 *#8250 Comprehending Text*

Genre: **Science Fiction**

READING FOCUS

- Analyzes and extracts information from a science-fiction text to answer literal, inferential, and applied questions

- Scans a science-fiction text to locate specific information

- Synthesizes information to compare characters from a text and to complete arguments for and against a debate

ANSWER KEY

Literal (Page 96)

1. His school was having its orientation day at the high school.

2. He wore clothes that were not as dull as those of the other students and did his hair differently from the other students in his group.

3. facial features

Inferential (Page 96)

1. Answers will vary.

2. Slade mentioned that his mom always told him that he was created just to be their "special" child.

3. Answers will vary. Possible answer(s): shocked, stunned, speechless; "David pulled himself free from his semi-catatonic state…"

Applied (Page 97)

1–2. Answers will vary.

3. Drawings will vary.

Applying Strategies (Page 98)

1. David—built wiry, determined, stubborn, fair hair, fair skin, blue eyes

   Slade—likes to stand out, confident, slightly built, brown hair, dark skin, brown eyes, spiked brown hair

2. Answers will vary. Possible answer(s):

   For—experiences influence your decisions; how others treat you can affect you; where a person lives has a big impact on his/her way of life

   Against—genetics determines your attributes; you are born with genetic predispositions; nature provides us with inborn abilities and traits

EXTENSIONS

- Students may enjoy reading the following science-fiction titles, some of which relate to the topic of adoption, increasing the numbers of endangered species, and family relationships:
  - *The Angel Factory* by Terence Blacker
  - *The Exchange Student* by Kate Gilmore
  - *Earthborn* by Sylvia Waugh
  - *Space Race* by Sylvia Waugh

MIRROR IMAGE

Name _____

Read the science-fiction story and answer the questions on the following pages.

David Roberts knew that he was different from other twelve-year-olds.

His parents had often told him that he had been specially chosen from a number of eggs and created just to be their "special" child. His hair and eye color resembled that of his adoptive parents, Marion and Jeff Roberts. He was slightly built like his dad, who was wiry like a runner, but he had his mom's determination and stubbornness. His parents encouraged and supported him in whatever he wanted to do. He knew that he was well loved.

The day came for David's high school orientation. He was to visit the local high school with his middle-school classmates so that the following year everything would not be so strange and overwhelming. Other local schools were also going to be present on the same day.

As the different school groups passed along their tour, the students critically assessed each other. They wondered whether any of the students would be in their classes next year and whether they would become friends or not.

David noticed a particular boy in one of the groups because he was being very closely supervised by a male teacher. The teacher addressed the boy as "Slade" whenever he needed to move the group along to the next venue. Slade was slightly built, had brown hair, dark skin, and brown eyes. However, his clothes were not as dull as those of the other students—he was the only student who wore an expensive denim jacket. He had taken a lot of time to spike his hair with gel. The sturdy army boots he wore were scuffed from constant use. He strutted along in his unusual garb as though he was wearing a badge of honor, completely oblivious to the teacher at his side and the stares and comments from students in other groups.

As the groups settled down for a lunch break, David noticed that Slade was sitting slightly apart from the other students in his group but closer to David's group. David talked to his friends as he demolished his lunch. During a lull in conversation, David looked around at the unfamiliar faces of students he would be attending high school with the following year. His eyes encountered Slade, who had turned to look around at the other students. Their eyes met and held. Each found himself spellbound by the apparition staring back.

David's hair was fair, but Slade's was dark. David's skin was fair, but Slade's was dark. David's eyes were blue, but Slade's were brown. The strange thing was that their facial features were exactly the same. It was almost like looking at a mirror image or a photo negative.

David pulled himself free from his semi-catatonic state and spoke to Slade.

"You're . . . You're just like me. You could be my twin!" stammered David.

"Yeah!" replied Slade. "Spooky! Strange! My mom always told me I was a little different—created just to be their 'special' child. Like I would believe garbage like that."

As David related the events of the day to his parents, he watched as a thoughtful expression came across his mother's face.

"You know . . . I recall Dr. Lewitt talking about his special interest in genetic engineering whenever I went for my tests," she said.

MIRROR IMAGE

Literal   Find the answers directly in the text.

1. Why was David at the high school?

   _____

   _____

2. Why did Slade stand out among the students in his group?

   _____

   _____

3. What was similar about David and Slade?

   _____

Inferential   Think about what the text says.

1. Why might Slade want his appearance to stand out among the other students?

   _____

   _____

2. What evidence in the text supports that Slade's parents cared for him as much as David's parents?

   _____

   _____

3. How do you think David felt when he saw someone who looked almost exactly like him? Use words from the text to support your answer.

   _____

   _____

   _____

MIRROR IMAGE

Applied   Use what you know about the text and your own experience.

1. Why do you think that children, even within one family, can be so different from each other?

_____

_____

_____

_____

_____

_____

2. How are you similar and different than your sibling(s)? If you do not have a sibling, compare yourself to your mom or dad or another family member you are close to.

_____

_____

_____

_____

3. In the space provided, draw your "mirror image."

Name _____

MIRROR IMAGE

Use the text on page 95 to complete the following activities.

1. In the boxes below, write descriptions to match the two boys in the text. Include aspects of their personalities and behavior.

David	Slade

2. There have been many arguments and debates about how much influence parents' genetic characteristics (nature) have on an individual's character, compared to the environment in which he/she is brought up (nurture). Use the information gained from the examples in the text and your own knowledge to write arguments (in bullet form) for and against the following:

Environment (Nurture) Shapes Most Aspects of an Individual's Character

For	Against
_____	_____
_____	_____
_____	_____
_____	_____
_____	_____
_____	_____

READING FOCUS

- Analyzes and extracts information from an autobiography to answer literal, inferential, and applied questions
- Uses synthesis to consider, compare, and analyze the effects of a major event in a writer's life

Genre: Autobiography

ANSWER KEY

Literal (Page 101)

1. a. Opinion   b. Fact   c. Fact   d. Opinion

2. 1826   he was born

   1835   his mother died

   1839   he was caught picking pockets, he was sentenced to transportation, or he was sent to Van Diemen's Land/Point Puer

   1846   he married Mary Clifton

Inferential (Page 101)

1. Answers should indicate that it was a major event in his life so far.

2. Answers will vary. Possible answer(s): bad memories of London, no family in London, created a life living in Hobart.

Applied (Page 102)

1–3. Answers will vary.

Applying Strategies (Page 103)

1. a. Answers will vary. Possible answer(s): experienced physical work, which made him stronger; learned a trade; experienced living in harsh conditions, which made him thankful for fair conditions; lived a life of prayer, church, work, and school so he had an education; constant threat of punishment at Point Puer may have taught him that actions have consequences.

   b. Answers will vary.

2–3. Answers will vary.

EXTENSIONS

- Students can find autobiographies of their favorite authors on the Internet.
- Using the Internet, students can research and learn about Tasmania.

LIFE OF A CONVICT

Name _____

Read the autobiography and answer the questions on the following pages.

I was born in London, England in 1826. My life as a young child was extremely unhappy. My mother was the only member of my family I knew, and she died when I was nine years old. I then lived on the streets, and stealing was a way of life. When I was 13 years old, I was caught picking pockets.

I thought I would be sent straight to prison, but instead I was sentenced to transportation. This meant that I would have to take a long sea voyage to a place called Van Diemen's Land—now known as Tasmania. Although I was frightened by this, I couldn't help feeling faintly hopeful. At least I wouldn't be on the streets anymore. Nothing could be worse than that. Or could it?

With hundreds of other convicts, I spent about five months on the ship traveling to Australia. I was miserable—it was cramped, dirty, and uncomfortable, and I was seasick a lot of the time. When we arrived in Van Diemen's Land, I was taken to a place called Point Puer. This was a prison for boys between the ages of 9 and 17. It was across the bay from Port Arthur, a men's prison, and consisted of a group of dilapidated buildings.

Soon after I arrived, I was assigned to a laboring gang, which meant physical work, such as cutting firewood and making bricks. After a few months, I was among a group of boys chosen to learn trades. My chosen trade was shoemaking. To my surprise, I quite enjoyed it. What I didn't enjoy was the harsh conditions at Point Puer. Life was an endless cycle of prayers, church, work, and school. The only real free time we had was on Saturday afternoons. There was also the constant threat of punishment. Any boy who misbehaved would suffer solitary confinement, reduced rations, or beatings. Not long after I arrived at Point Puer, I spent 10 days in solitary confinement for fighting

with another boy. It was so terrifying that from then on I was mostly well behaved. However, like many of the other boys, I stole food and tools to trade with the men who arrived each day from Port Arthur to bring us water and food. I was never caught, although some of the other boys were.

Finally, after two years at Point Puer, I was given my ticket-of-leave. I went to live in nearby Hobart and soon found work with a shoemaker. When I was 20, I married a young woman named Mary Clifton, and we had a son named Matthew. Life became much better. I eventually bought my own shoe shop.

I now have a happy life living in Hobart. I have no wish to go back to England. Matthew doesn't know about my former life yet, but one day I plan to tell him. He is now exactly the same age I was when I left England. I know that his life will be better than mine.

LIFE OF A CONVICT

| **Literal** | Find the answers directly in the text. |

1. Choose **Fact** or **Opinion** for each of these statements.

   a. The writer was a good pickpocket. ☐ Fact ☐ Opinion

   b. Tasmania was once called Van Diemen's Land. ☐ Fact ☐ Opinion

   c. The writer thought that life in Australia would
      be better than life in London. ☐ Fact ☐ Opinion

   d. Working for a shoemaker in Hobart was an
      excellent opportunity for the writer. ☐ Fact ☐ Opinion

2. Write an event that took place in the writer's life for each year.

   1826 _____

   1835 _____

   1839 _____

   1846 _____

| **Inferential** | Think about what the text says. |

1. Why do you think that most of the writer's autobiography is about his time in Point Puer?

   _____

   _____

2. List three possible reasons why the writer may not want to go back to London.

   • _____

     _____

   • _____

     _____

   • _____

     _____

LIFE OF A CONVICT

| **Applied** | Use what you know about the text and your own experience. |

1. Imagine you are Matthew. Your father has just told you about his convict life for the first time. Write what your response might be. Include any questions you have for him.

_____

_____

_____

_____

_____

_____

_____

2. Do you think the boys at Point Puer should have been allowed more free time? Give reasons to support your answer.

_____

_____

_____

_____

3. If you were at Point Puer, what trade would you have chosen? Why?

_____

_____

_____

_____

_____

_____

_____

Name _____

LIFE OF A CONVICT

Most events in our lives have positive and negative aspects. For example, failing a test might be negative because you might have to retake the test, but also positive because it helps you to understand what areas you need to work on. Using the text from page 100, think about the writer's experience of going to Point Puer for two years.

1. **a.** List the ways you think Point Puer might have impacted his life. They can be positive or negative.

    _____

    _____

    _____

    _____

    _____

    _____

    b. Write a **P** next to each positive effect and an **N** next to each negative effect that you wrote.

2. Mark the scale to show your view of the overall effect of Point Puer on the writer's life.

Positive								**Negative**

3. Based on your answers, write a short speech from the writer's point of view, explaining how Point Puer affected his life. Indicate whether it had more positive or negative effects.

    _____

    _____

    _____

    _____

    _____

    _____

    _____

    _____

    _____

    _____

    _____

READING FOCUS

- Analyzes and extracts information from two poems to answer literal, inferential, and applied questions
- Uses summarizing and paraphrasing to show comprehension of two poems

---

ANSWER KEY

Literal (Page 106)

1. True   2. True   3. True   4. True

Inferential (Page 106)

1. parent annoyer
2. peer satisfier, crowd pleaser, mood lifter, listener attractor, ego expander, stress slapper
3. parent confuser
4. shopping provider, upgrade collector, energy user, virus attractor

Applied (Page 107)

1–2. Answers will vary.

Applying Strategies (Page 108)

1. **Computers**

   Advantages—word processor, information researcher, game player, layout organizer, design creator, email dispenser, comrade communicator, email receiver, knowledge gatherer, shopping provider, technology utilizer, buddy networker, data storer, program runner, information presenter, homework helper, image manipulator, music downloader, upgrade collector

   Disadvantages—telephone interrupter, parent confuser, upgrade collector, energy user, virus attractor, human contact inhibitor

   Bass Guitars

   Advantages—melody maker, rhythm keeper, peer satisfier, crowd pleaser, mood lifter, listener attractor, ego expander, stress slapper

   Disadvantages—parent annoyer, noise maker, neck stretcher, palm strainer

2. Answers will vary.

EXTENSIONS

- Students may wish to investigate examples of kennings found on the Internet in stories such as *Beowulf*, or used in book or movie titles, such as *Whale Rider* and *The Bone Collector*.
- Another more unusual form of poetry is the "tanka," which is similar to haiku. Students may enjoy researching and writing both of these forms as well as some kennings of their own.

MY BASS GUITAR AND MY COMPUTER

Name _____

Read the poems below, which are written in a poetic form called *kennings*, and answer the questions on the following pages.

My Computer Is . . .

Word processor, information researcher,

game player, layout organizer,

design creator, email dispenser,

comrade communicator,

email receiver, knowledge gatherer,

shopping provider, technology utilizer,

telephone interrupter, buddy networker,

data storer, program runner,

information presenter, homework helper,

image manipulator, music downloader,

parent confuser, upgrade collector,

energy user, virus attractor,

human contact inhibitor!

My Bass Guitar Is . . .

Melody maker, rhythm keeper,

chord changer, string strummer,

beat bellower, song accompanier,

sound echoer, vibration boomer,

noise maker, finger flicker,

hand mover, arm placer,

head banger, leg knocker,

neck stretcher, palm strainer,

air stirrer, floor shaker,

parent annoyer, peer satisfier,

crowd pleaser, mood lifter,

listener attractor, ego expander,

stress slapper!

MY BASS GUITAR AND MY COMPUTER

Literal   Find the answers directly in the text.

Read each sentence. Decide if each statement is **True** or **False**.

1. A bass guitar can keep rhythm and beat and
accompany a song.   ☐ True   ☐ False

2. The bass guitar can annoy parents   ☐ True   ☐ False

3. Computers can be networked.   ☐ True   ☐ False

4. There are some advantages and disadvantages
to using computers.   ☐ True   ☐ False

Inferential   Think about what the text says.

Write some words from the poems that show the following:

1. Bass guitars are not popular with everyone.

_____

2. Playing the bass guitar can build the player's self-esteem and confidence.

_____

_____

3. Some people have difficulty using computers.

_____

4. Computers can be expensive to own and use.

_____

_____

MY BASS GUITAR AND MY COMPUTER

Applied   Use what you know about the text and your own experience.

1. Write sentences to answer the following questions, making sure that you give reasons or explanations for your opinions.

   a. How can learning to play a musical instrument help a person's health and well-being?

   _____

   _____

   b. Is today's society too dependent upon computers?

   _____

   _____

   c. Has the invention of devices such as the computer and the bass guitar made it more difficult for people to get along with each other?

   _____

   _____

2. Use the boxes below to add additional lines to the poems about bass guitars and computers.

Bass Guitars	Computers

MY BASS GUITAR AND MY COMPUTER

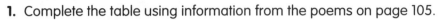

Summarizing

1. Complete the table using information from the poems on page 105.

Computers	
Advantages	**Disadvantages**

Bass Guitars	
Advantages	**Disadvantages**

2. Write a paragraph for each poem to summarize the main information given by the poet about bass guitars and computers.

Paraphrasing

Bass Guitars

_____
_____
_____
_____
_____
_____
_____
_____

Computers

_____
_____
_____
_____
_____
_____
_____
_____

Common Core State Standards

Standards Correlations

Each lesson meets one or more of the following Common Core State Standards ©Copyright 2010. National Governors Association Center for Best Practices and Council of Chief State School Officers. All rights reserved. For more information about the Common Core State Standards, go to *http://www.corestandards.org/* or *http://www.teachercreated.com/standards.*

Grade 7 Correlations

Reading Literature/Fiction Text Standards	Text Title	Pages
Key Ideas and Details		
ELA.RL.7.1 Cite several pieces of textual evidence to support analysis of what the text says explicitly as well as inferences drawn from the text.	Elf Boy Meets Superman®	9–13
	Between Outer-Earth and Inner-Earth	14–18
	Krishna and the Serpent	29–33
	The Children of Lir	34–38
	The Mystery of the Locked Door	39–43
	The Rescue	44–48
	The Wizard	49–53
	Hex and the Captive City of Hur	64–68
	The Secret Book	69–73
	Don't Count Your Chickens!	74–78
	Mirror Image	94–98
	My Bass Guitar and My Computer	104–108
ELA.RL.7.2 Determine a theme or central idea of a text and analyze its development over the course of the text; provide an objective summary of the text.	Elf Boy Meets Superman®	9–13
	The Children of Lir	34–38
	The Mystery of the Locked Door	39–43
	The Wizard	49–53
	Don't Count Your Chickens!	74–78
	Mirror Image	94–98
	My Bass Guitar and My Computer	104–108
ELA.RL.7.3 Analyze how particular elements of a story or drama interact (e.g., how setting shapes the characters or plot).	Elf Boy Meets Superman®	9–13
	Krishna and the Serpent	29–33
	The Children of Lir	34–38
	Hex and the Captive City of Hur	64–68
	The Secret Book	69–73
	Don't Count Your Chickens!	74–78
Craft and Structure		
ELA.RL.7.4 Determine the meaning of words and phrases as they are used in a text, including figurative and connotative meanings; analyze the impact of rhymes and other repetitions of sounds (e.g., alliteration) on a specific verse or stanza of a poem or section of a story or drama.	Elf Boy Meets Superman®	9–13
	Krishna and the Serpent	29–33
	The Mystery of the Locked Door	39–43
	The Rescue	44–48
	Hex and the Captive City of Hur	64–68
	The Secret Book	69–73
	Don't Count Your Chickens!	74–78
	My Bass Guitar and My Computer	104–108
ELA.RL.7.5 Analyze how a drama's or poem's form or structure (e.g., soliloquy, sonnet) contributes to its meaning.	The Mystery of the Locked Door	39–43
	The Wizard	49–53
	The Secret Book	69–73
	Don't Count Your Chickens!	74–78
ELA.RL.7.6 Analyze how an author develops and contrasts the points of view of different characters or narrators in a text.	The Children of Lir	34–38
	The Mystery of the Locked Door	39–43
	The Secret Book	69–73

Common Core State Standards *(cont.)*

Reading Literature/Fiction Text Standards *(cont.)*	Text Title	Pages
Range of Reading and Level of Text Complexity		
ELA.RL.7.10 By the end of the year, read and comprehend literature, including stories, dramas, and poems, in the grades 6–8 text complexity band proficiently, with scaffolding as needed at the high end of the range.	Elf Boy Meets Superman®	9–13
	Between Outer–Earth and Inner–Earth	14–18
	Krishna and the Serpent	29–33
	The Children of Lir	34–38
	The Mystery of the Locked Door	39–43
	The Rescue	44–48
	The Wizard	49–53
	Hex and the Captive City of Hur	64–68
	The Secret Book	69–73
	Don't Count Your Chickens!	74–78
	Mirror Image	94–98
	My Bass Guitar and My Computer	104–108

Reading Informational Text/Nonfiction Standards	Text Title	Pages
Key Ideas and Details		
ELA.RI.7.1 Cite several pieces of textual evidence to support analysis of what the text says explicitly as well as inferences drawn from the text.	Lucky Jim	19–23
	Amazing Amy!	24–28
	School Timetable	54–58
	Two Letters	59–63
	Irish Legends	79–83
	A Surfing Champion	84–88
	Bare Trees Baffle Local Farmer	89–93
	Life of a Convict	99–103
ELA.RI.7.2 Determine two or more central ideas in a text and analyze their development over the course of the text; provide an objective summary of the text.	Irish Legends	79–83
	A Surfing Champion	84–88
ELA.RI.7.3 Analyze the interactions between individuals, events, and ideas in a text (e.g., how ideas influence individuals or events, or how individuals influence ideas or events).	Lucky Jim	19–23
	Amazing Amy!	24–28
	Two Letters	59–63
	Irish Legends	79–83
	A Surfing Champion	84–88
	Bare Trees Baffle Local Farmer	89–93
	Life of a Convict	99–103
Craft and Structure		
ELA.RI.7.4 Determine the meaning of words and phrases as they are used in a text, including figurative, connotative, and technical meanings; analyze the impact of a specific word choice on meaning and tone.	Lucky Jim	19–23
	Amazing Amy!	24–28
	Two Letters	59–63
	Irish Legends	79–83
	A Surfing Champion	84–88
	Bare Trees Baffle Local Farmer	89–93
ELA.RI.7.5 Analyze the structure an author uses to organize a text, including how the major sections contribute to the whole and to the development of the ideas.	School Timetable	54–58
	Two Letters	59–63
ELA.RI.7.6 Determine an author's point of view or purpose in a text and analyze how the author distinguishes his or her position from that of others.	Life of a Convict	99–103
Integration of Knowledge and Ideas		
ELA.RI.7.9 Analyze how two or more authors writing about the same topic shape their presentations of key information by emphasizing different evidence or advancing different interpretations of facts.	Two Letters	59–63

Reading Informational Text/Nonfiction Standards *(cont.)*	Text Title	Pages
Range of Reading and Level of Text Complexity		
ELA.RI.7.10 By the end of the year, read and comprehend literary nonfiction in the grades 6–8 text complexity band proficiently, with scaffolding as needed at the high end of the range.	Lucky Jim	19–23
	Amazing Amy!	24–28
	School Timetable	54–58
	Two Letters	59–63
	Irish Legends	79–83
	A Surfing Champion	84–88
	Bare Trees Baffle Local Farmer	89–93
	Life of a Convict	99–103

Grade 8 Correlations

Reading Literature/Fiction Text Standards	Text Title	Pages
Key Ideas and Details		
ELA.RL.8.1 Cite the textual evidence that most strongly supports an analysis of what the text says explicitly as well as inferences drawn from the text.	Elf Boy Meets Superman®	9–13
	Between Outer-Earth and Inner-Earth	14–18
	Krishna and the Serpent	29–33
	The Children of Lir	34–38
	The Mystery of the Locked Door	39–43
	The Rescue	44–48
	The Wizard	49–53
	Hex and the Captive City of Hur	64–68
	The Secret Book	69–73
	Don't Count Your Chickens!	74–78
	Mirror Image	94–98
	My Bass Guitar and My Computer	104–108
ELA.RL.8.2 Determine a theme or central idea of a text and analyze its development over the course of the text, including its relationship to the characters, setting, and plot; provide an objective summary of the text.	Elf Boy Meets Superman®	9–13
	The Children of Lir	34–38
	The Mystery of the Locked Door	39–43
	The Wizard	49–53
	Don't Count Your Chickens!	74–78
	Mirror Image	94–98
	My Bass Guitar and My Computer	104–108
ELA.RL.8.3 Analyze how particular lines of dialogue or incidents in a story or drama propel the action, reveal aspects of a character, or provoke a decision.	Elf Boy Meets Superman®	9–13
	Krishna and the Serpent	29–33
	The Children of Lir	34–38
	Hex and the Captive City of Hur	64–68
	The Secret Book	69–73
	Don't Count Your Chickens!	74–78
Craft and Structure		
ELA.RL.8.4 Determine the meaning of words and phrases as they are used in a text, including figurative and connotative meanings; analyze the impact of specific word choices on meaning and tone, including analogies or allusions to other texts.	Elf Boy Meets Superman®	9–13
	Krishna and the Serpent	29–33
	The Mystery of the Locked Door	39–43
	The Rescue	44–48
	Hex and the Captive City of Hur	64–68
	The Secret Book	69–73
	Don't Count Your Chickens!	74–78
	My Bass Guitar and My Computer	104–108
Range of Reading and Level of Text Complexity		
ELA.RL.8.10 By the end of the year, read and comprehend literature, including stories, dramas, and poems, at the high end of grades 6–8 text complexity band independently and proficiently.	Elf Boy Meets Superman®	9–13
	Between Outer-Earth and Inner-Earth	14–18
	Krishna and the Serpent	29–33

Common Core State Standards *(cont.)*

Reading Literature/Fiction Text Standards *(cont.)*	Text Title	Pages
Range of Reading and Level of Text Complexity *(cont.)*		
ELA.RL.8.10 *(cont.)*	The Children of Lir	34–38
	The Mystery of the Locked Door	39–43
	The Rescue	44–48
	The Wizard	49–53
	Hex and the Captive City of Hur	64–68
	The Secret Book	69–73
	Don't Count Your Chickens!	74–78
	Mirror Image	94–98
	My Bass Guitar and My Computer	104–108

Reading Informational Text/Nonfiction Standards	Text Title	Pages
Key Ideas and Details		
ELA.RI.8.1 Cite the textual evidence that most strongly supports an analysis of what the text says explicitly as well as inferences drawn from the text.	Lucky Jim	19–23
	Amazing Amy!	24–28
	School Timetable	54–58
	Two Letters	59–63
	Irish Legends	79–83
	A Surfing Champion	84–88
	Bare Trees Baffle Local Farmer	89–93
	Life of a Convict	99–103
ELA.RI.8.2 Determine a central idea of a text and analyze its development over the course of the text, including its relationship to supporting ideas; provide an objective summary of the text.	Irish Legends	79–83
	A Surfing Champion	84–88
ELA.RI.8.3 Analyze how a text makes connections among and distinctions between individuals, ideas, or events (e.g., through comparisons, analogies, or categories).	Amazing Amy!	24–28
	School Timetable	54–58
	Two Letters	59–63
	Irish Legends	79–83
	A Surfing Champion	84–88
	Life of a Convict	99–103
Craft and Structure		
ELA.RI.8.4 Determine the meaning of words and phrases as they are used in a text, including figurative, connotative, and technical meanings; analyze the impact of specific word choices on meaning and tone, including analogies or allusions to other texts.	Lucky Jim	19–23
	Amazing Amy!	24–28
	Two Letters	59–63
	Irish Legends	79–83
	A Surfing Champion	84–88
	Bare Trees Baffle Local Farmer	89–93
ELA.RI.8.5 Analyze in detail the structure of a specific paragraph in a text, including the role of particular sentences in developing and refining a key concept.	School Timetable	54–58
	Two Letters	59–63
ELA.RI.8.6 Determine an author's point of view or purpose in a text and analyze how the author acknowledges and responds to conflicting evidence or viewpoints.	Life of a Convict	99–103
Range of Reading and Level of Text Complexity		
ELA.RI.8.10 By the end of the year, read and comprehend literary nonfiction at the high end of the grades 6–8 text complexity band independently and proficiently.	Lucky Jim	19–23
	Amazing Amy!	24–28
	School Timetable	54–58
	Two Letters	59–63
	Irish Legends	79–83
	A Surfing Champion	84–88
	Bare Trees Baffle Local Farmer	89–93
	Life of a Convict	99–103